TEN BOYS WHO MADE HISTORY

LIGHT KEEPERS

Irene Howat

CF4·K

Copyright © Christian Focus Publications 2003
Reprinted 2004, 2005, 2007, 2008, 2010, 2012, 2014, 2016
Paperback ISBN: 978-1-85792-836-5
E-pub ISBN: 978-1-84550-844-9
Mobi ISBN: 978-1-84550-845-6

Published by Christian Focus Publications,
Geanies House, Fearn, Tain, Ross-shire,
IV20 1TW, Scotland, Great Britain.
www.christianfocus.com
e-mail:info@christianfocus.com

Cover Design by Alister MacInnes
Cover Illustration by Elena Temporin,
Milan Illustrations Agency
Printed and bound by Nørhaven, Denmark

All incidents retold in these stories are based on true situations. Where specific information about childhood incidents has been unobtainable the author has written these paragraphs using other information concerning family life, hobbies, home life and relationships, freely available as well as appropriate historical source material.

Cover illustration: This depicts Robert Murray McCheyne as a young lad. He was a very active child despite his ill health. In later years he would practice gymnastics and the parallel bars amongst other things. He even hurt himself quite severely when showing a young boy how to do a particular gymnastic manoeuvre on some poles in the garden. Read all about this in chapter 5.

for
Ali and Mo

Contents

Samuel Rutherford

Samuel stood looking at the burn marks on the wall high above him.

'Jedburgh Abbey was burned down by the Earl of Surrey's army about ninety years ago,' his teacher told the boys. 'In 1523, to be exact. Since then it has been occupied several times. In fact, from what is left it is hard to imagine how magnificent the building once was.'

'Sir,' said Samuel. 'Was the church roof originally much higher? It seems so low compared with the rest of the building.'

'Good thinking,' the teacher said. 'The roof was very high before the great fire. But rather than replace it after it was burned down, it was lowered and internal walls were built to make the church smaller. Of course, the Latiners' Alley, where the school meets, was originally inside the great abbey.'

The teacher surveyed his pupils.

'How,' he asked the youngest boy, 'did the Latiners' Alley get its name?'

The boy looked puzzled, then he grinned.

'Sir,' he said. 'Is it because that's where we learn Latin?'

'Quite right,' smiled the teacher, and that's what we're going to do now.'

Glancing all around him, Samuel tried to imagine what Jedburgh Abbey must have looked like before the Earl of Surrey's army did their worst.

As they walked home to the village of Nisbet after school that afternoon, Samuel and his brothers discussed what they had been told.

'Will we go by the road or along the Jed Water?' James asked.

'Let's go by the river,' suggested George.

The three brothers left the road and dropped to the right towards the riverbank.

'I like history,' Samuel commented. 'It makes sense of things.'

'Let's pretend to be the Scots' army spying on the Earl of Surrey's troops,' George said. 'I reckon we could get all the way to Bonjedward without being seen from the road if we kept to the bushes.'

His brothers thought that sounded a very satisfactory way of returning home after a day at school. For over a mile they dodged from bush to bush and rock to rock. Even though they could see people walking on the main road, and on the track to the other side of the Jed Water, nobody called their names and shouted hello. They were very pleased with themselves, if a little dusty and covered in grass.

'Just quarter of a mile to go,' whispered James, as they neared Bonjedward.

'What did you say?' asked a voice from the far side of the copse they were hiding in.

The boys felt like burst balloons. They had been so pleased with their spy act, and just before reaching the village they had been discovered. An old man came round the copse to where the boys were crouching.

'Hiding, are you?' he asked.

Samuel decided it was better to explain what they'd been playing at than to seem very foolish. Old Mr Ker smiled when he heard their story.

'I'm going home to Bonjedward,' he told them. 'And if you walk with me I'll tell you some more of the history of the area. And it's every bit as exciting as the Earl of

Surrey's attack on the Abbey, because I saw it with my own two eyes.'

The boys got to their feet immediately, and joined the old man on his walk along the river bank.

'When I was a boy,' he said. 'There was a great battle just four miles from here, at Ancrum. I was six years old at the time, and I'm 76 now, but I remember it as though it was yesterday. King Henry of England sent an army that landed at the port of Leith before entering Edinburgh, where he set the city on fire. It was said that the fires didn't go out for four days.'

The boys' eyes danced with excitement.

'His army marched south, and some Scots families joined them on the way.'

'Why did they do that?' George asked.

'I suppose it was join them or be killed by them,' Mr Ker explained. 'By February 1545 the great army had reached Ancrum Moor and camped there. Do you know where the battle site is?'

'Yes,' James told him. 'It's just three miles up the road from here.'

Pleased that they knew where the battle site was, Mr Ker went on with his story. 'News went round that the English army had set fire to the Tower of Broomhill, burning to death an old woman, her family and her servants, who were locked inside. So the Scots forces were in a real mood for battle. They were an odd assortment of men, but rage drove them on. With cries of "Remember Broomhouse" they surged towards the English. Very cleverly they timed the battle for late afternoon when the setting sun would dazzle their enemies' eyes. The Scots fought with a fury and scattered their enemy, or what was left of them, for 800 English troops died on Ancrum Moor.'

The old man, seeing that his audience was captivated by his tale, looked for the perfect finishing line.

'That was my earliest memory,' he said. 'The cries of "Remember Broomhouse" and the clash of swords. Your earliest memories will be tamer than that, I'm sure.'

James and George looked at their brother, wondering if he would tell Mr Ker his story.

'Would you like to know my earliest memory?' Samuel asked.

'I would indeed,' said the old man.

'There is a well in the village of Nisbet,' the lad said. 'The water in it is about three feet deep. I was playing there with my friends one day when I sat on the edge of the well and fell in. They ran for help, knowing I would drown if I didn't get out. But while they were away a lovely man dressed in white came and pulled me out of

11

the well. I was safe on the grass beside the well when my friends came back with help.'

'A lovely man dressed in white,' Mr Ker repeated. 'Who was he then?'

'I didn't know him,' Samuel said.

'Was he an angel?' asked the old man.

Samuel shook his head and smiled. 'I didn't know him,' he repeated. 'But that's my earliest memory.'

By the time the boy had told his story, the four of them had reached the village of Bonjedward. The boys left Mr Ker there and walked the last stretch of the Water of Jed to where it joined the River Teviot. Then they turned east, and walked the mile along the grassy bank of the Teviot to their home, passing the well on the way.

By the time Samuel was 17, he was a student in Edinburgh. Soon after he graduated in 1621, he was made a professor. But he resigned just four years later and spent his time studying theology. In 1627, he moved to the parish of Anwoth and became minister there. We don't know when Samuel became a Christian, but his heart was just full of love for the Lord Jesus by the time he had grown up.

'What do you think of the Solway coast?' one of his church members asked, not long after he arrived in the area.

'It's a fine part of Scotland,' Samuel told him. 'And the church is in a beautiful place, with the hill beside it, trees around it, and the sea within walking distance. I already love the place, and I'm growing to love the people too.'

The man was about to say more, but Samuel excused himself.

'There are two lads over there herding the sheep. I'd like to talk to them.'

With that Samuel was off to make friends with the youth of his congregation.

The man watched him go. 'Rutherford's nothing to look at,' he thought, 'just a little fair-haired man. But there is something about him I like.'

'Hello there,' Samuel called out to the boys. 'I'm the new minister. What are your names?'

'I'm Thomas,' one answered.

'And I'm Archie,' said the other.

'Well, Thomas and Archie,' Rutherford smiled. 'I've got news for you.'

The boys looked interested.

'The Lord Jesus himself knew about herding sheep,' he told them. 'He's the best shepherd of all, and he loves you both more than you'll ever know.'

The boys liked their new minister immediately.

'Goodbye, boys,' Samuel said. 'It's good to meet you.'

'Mr Rutherford is different from many ministers,' commented a local farmer.

'In what way?' asked the farmer's brother, who was visiting him.

'Most ministers preach about hell's fire and try to frighten us into becoming Christians.'

'So they do,' the other man said. 'And there's nothing wrong with that.'

The farmer ignored what had been said.

'Mr Rutherford preaches about the love of God rather than the fires of hell. He makes God's love sound so ... so...so lovely.'

'Lovely!' his brother said crossly. 'That message will not make much of an impact. You need hell shouted from the pulpit to make people listen.'

'We do listen to Mr Rutherford,' the farmer told his brother. 'It's almost as if he wants us to fall in love with the Lord Jesus.'

'I've never heard anything so sloppy in all my life!' the other man announced.

But the farmer knew that he had fallen in love with Jesus, and his life had been changed completely.

Samuel worked hard in Anwoth, even though things were far from easy for him. His young wife died after a year of illness, and two of his children died there too. In 1636, he published a book showing that we are saved through God's grace and special choice. Unfortunately the church authorities didn't like that at all and he was called before the High Court! The court exiled him to Aberdeen.

'I long to be in Anwoth,' Samuel thought, as he looked out over the grey granite buildings of Aberdeen. 'I long to see my dear people and to tell them about the love of Jesus.'

He sat at his table and began to write a letter to one of his congregation. It was the first of many letters that went from Aberdeen to Anwoth. And so beautiful were his letters, and so full of love, that people kept them and they were collected into a book which is still being read today, over three-and-a-half centuries after they were written!

Scotland in the 1630s was in great confusion. The king was trying to make the church in Scotland like the church south of the border, and not everyone was happy about it. In 1638, there were so many comings and goings that Samuel was able to slip out of Aberdeen and make his way back to Anwoth.

'Every mile is a mile nearer Anwoth,' he thought, as he travelled from the northeast of Scotland to the southwest. 'And every mile is a mile nearer my dear people.'

But Samuel was not back in Anwoth long before the Church of Scotland held a General Assembly and broke free from the king's church once again. Not only that, but the Assembly appointed Samuel Rutherford as a Professor of Theology in St Andrews University.

It was with a very sad heart that he said goodbye to the people he loved, and rode away from Anwoth.

Five years later, Samuel found himself in London. A great assembly of ministers was held there, and he was invited to join them. They had the job of working out exactly what the Bible taught, and putting the teachings together in a book that became known as the Westminster Confession of Faith. They also compiled the Larger and Shorter Catechisms. All of these are still in use today!

'It's good to be home in Scotland,' Samuel told his colleagues, when he arrived back from London. 'I much prefer the fresh sea air to the awful smell of the River Thames.'

'Have you made plans for what you'll do now?' he was asked.

Rutherford nodded. 'Yes,' he said. 'I'll teach my students, of course. But there's a book that needs writing, and I think I'm the one to write it.'

'What will it be about?' queried his colleague.

Samuel thought for a moment before answering. 'It will be about the relationship between the king and the church. God is the King of Kings, and the king of the country needs to know that.'

The other university teacher shook his head.

'Are you wise to think of writing a book on that subject?' he asked. 'It won't be popular.'

He did write his book, and the king didn't like it one little bit. Rutherford was charged with treason in 1661 and summoned to appear in court. Samuel, who was by then very unwell, refused to go. When the summons was delivered to him, he answered the messenger, 'I must answer my first summons; and before your day arrives, I will be where few kings and great folk come.' By the day that had been set for his trial, Samuel Rutherford had answered God's summons to go to heaven, where he met the King of Kings, whom he had loved deeply and served faithfully.

Fact File: *The Covenanters.*
During Samuel's life there was a lot of disagreement between the king and the church in Scotland about the way that they should worship God. Many of those who disagreed with the king were persecuted by government soldiers. These people were called the Covenanters, because some of their leaders had signed a protest about what the king was doing. This protest was called The National Covenant. It said that they would obey God rather than the king. The Covenant was signed in Greyfriars Kirkyard in Edinburgh.

Keynote: Samuel got into a lot of trouble because he resisted the king's attempts to control the church. He was willing to go through this because he knew that God was the King of kings and was more important than any human leader. There are still countries where Christians are persecuted. They know that God is more important than any government. Although Samuel suffered greatly, God gave him the strength and help that he needed to get through the difficult times.

Think: Samuel believed that God is the King of kings. That means that he is most important, and that we should all do what he tells us in the Bible. When we don't do this, we sin. Sin displeases God. Jesus came so that we could be forgiven for our sins, but also so that we can learn to obey God more and more each day. Do you try to obey God? Who can help you to find out more about what God wants you to do?

Prayer: Lord Jesus, thank you for your love. You are perfect, and in charge of everything. Thank you for those who suffered in the past so that we would be able to worship you in the way that the Bible tells us. Help those Christians who are suffering for you today. Amen.

John Owen

The two boys stood side by side on the bank of the stream.

'I dare you,' William said to his friend.

John looked at the rushing water. Then he looked behind him to see how good a run he would get at it.

'OK,' he said. 'I dare you too.'

Taking one last look at the stream to find a good solid edge from which to leap, John turned and strode back over the rise of grass.

'Ready?' asked William.

John nodded.

'Go!'

John Owen pelted down the rise and over the grass to the stream. Measuring his paces perfectly, he arrived at the water's edge on a left stride, catapulted over, and just managed to reach solid ground with his right foot before throwing himself forward and landing flat-out on the grass. Grinning from ear to ear he lay there, not turning to

21

watch the inevitable, just enjoying imagining it. He could hear his friend thudding down the grass bank. He enjoyed the seconds of silence when he was in the air, and the anticipation of the almighty splash that would surely follow. And he wasn't disappointed.

'You all right?' he asked, rolling over on to his back, all the better to see William stagger out of the stream, dripping from the top of his head to the soles of his feet.

'You've been practising!' the soaking lad fumed.

Scrambling to his feet, John pulled off his jacket and threw it to his friend.

'I'm sorry,' he said. 'But I couldn't resist it when you dared me.'

By the time they'd got back to the village of Stadham, they were the best of friends again.

When they parted, John raced through the village to his home.

'Where's Dad?' he called, as he went in the door.

His mother looked up from her mending. 'He's in his room working on Sunday's sermons,' she said. 'You'd better not disturb him.'

John grumped, and sat down at the table.

'Have you finished the work Dad gave you to do?' his mother asked.

Looking guilty, the boy admitted he had not.

His mother tried not to smile. 'I suggest you get out your books and do it before your father comes through. He may be your kindly minister, but he's your schoolmaster too.'

Taking his books from a shelf on the wall, John settled at the table and began his mathematics. It wasn't that he didn't like working, far from it. But it was a glorious day, one that just begged him to run and jump and kick stones around with his friends.

'Do I need to go to school in Oxford?' John asked his father, later that day. 'There are still loads of things I could learn from you.'

His father, who was the minister in the small village of Stadham, explained that a teacher in Oxford, a Mr Sylvester, would be able to teach him much more.

Having lost that argument, John tried a different one.

'Oxford is miles away,' he said. 'And I won't know anyone there.'

Mr Owen smiled. John really was stretching it! Oxford was only six miles away. His son had one last shot.

'There'll be nothing for a boy to do in Oxford!' he said, though he was already feeling quite excited by the challenge.

Smiling broadly, Mr Owen assured his son that there would be plenty to do in Oxford. There would be mathematics, Latin, Greek, history, English grammar, and plenty else besides.

'And there's the River Thames,' John's father concluded. 'It may not be the mighty river it is when it flows through London, but it is still deep enough to soak your friends.'

John's neck grew red, then the blush crept up his face, until he could not help but smile.

'You heard about William?' the boy asked.

His father grinned back. 'Yes,' he replied. 'I heard about William!'

So young John Owen left home for Oxford, and Mr Sylvester's school, where he studied hard and did very well indeed.

In November 1631, when he was just 15 years old, John Owen became a student at Queen's College, Oxford.

'I'm really enjoying my studies,' he wrote home to his father and mother, towards the end of his first year. 'But it is very hard work. I only allow myself 4 hours sleep a night. But in case you think your son's life is all work and no play, occasionally I take time off to practise my jumping, throwing the bar and bell-ringing. Of course, I have my regular music lessons, which give me a break from my books. By the way, did I tell you that my music teacher taught the king to play the flute?'

During John's student years, what he had learned at home about the Lord Jesus became real to him, and he knew that Jesus was his Saviour. At the same time there were changes in the university that he found impossible to live with.

'How can the Chancellor do these things?' he asked himself. 'This is a Protestant university, yet he's bringing in all kinds of Romanist things. The chapel service last Sunday was a Mass!'

John agonised over this, and discussed it with his friends.

'Owen!' a fellow student called after him one day. 'I want to speak to you.'

The two young men walked along the bank of the Thames.

'Have you heard the news?' John's friend asked, then rushed on to tell what he had heard. 'Anyone objecting to the Romanist innovations the Chancellor is bringing in is to be expelled from the University!'

Suspecting that might happen, John had already thought the issue through.

'In that case I'd better pack my things and go home,' he said. 'Because what the Chancellor is bringing in is against what the Bible teaches, and I'm not prepared to accept it.'

On leaving Oxford, John Owen became a private chaplain for a time before moving to London. He also became an author.

'What a year 1643 has been,' he told a friend that December. 'In July I moved here to Fordham in Essex, and in the few months since then I met and married Mary.' He grinned. 'I think coming to Fordham was a good move!'

John grew to know the area around Fordham very well as he visited the homes of his people. From house to house he went in the hamlets round the parish, from Rose Green to Gallows Green and from there to the quaintly named Seven Stars Green, then east to Eight Ash Green. Sometimes, as he crossed and recrossed the River Colne that flowed right through his parish, he smiled at the memory of his exploits with William back home in Stadham.

'Here's the minister coming to catechise us,' children called to their parents, when they saw him coming.

The parents and children would go into their homes and listen to John Owen's teaching then answer the questions he asked them on the Christian faith.

'I've been asked to preach before Parliament,' John told his wife, in the spring of 1646.

'You'll only do that once in your life!' Mary said, smiling at the thought of what her husband had been asked to do. 'It's the people of Fordham who'll hear most of your sermons.'

But just a few months later, the people of Fordham said goodbye to their minister, as he moved five miles away to Coggelshall. Soon he had a congregation of nearly 2000 people which gathered in the market-town to hear him preach.

These were troubled times in England, and John found himself in the centre of things. King Charles I was accused of being a traitor, tyrant and murderer. At a trial before the High Court of Justice he was found guilty and sentenced to death. On 31st January 1649, the king was beheaded. The following day, John preached before Parliament. He was back there again three months later. On that occasion, Oliver Cromwell heard him preach. No king succeeded Charles I, and Oliver Cromwell became the military ruler of the country. Although he made some bad mistakes, Cromwell was a Christian, and he liked Owen's preaching. The day after Cromwell heard John preach, the two men met again.

'Sir,' said Cromwell, 'you are the man I want to get to know.'

'That will be more to my advantage than to yours,' answered Owen.

Taking John by the arm, Cromwell spoke to him quietly and urgently.

'I'm leaving with my troops for Ireland soon,' he said. 'And I want you with me as chaplain.'

On the ship to Ireland, John Owen talked over the events of the previous day with one of the soldiers.

'I've never seen anything like it,' the soldier said. 'Twelve thousand soldiers spending a whole day in prayer, fasting and reading their Bibles, apart from when they were listening to three sermons being preached.'

'It was a day to remember,' Owen said. 'There's never before been one like it.'

Cromwell's troops did what they set out to do in Ireland, and then returned home. The following year they were mobilised again, and headed north to Scotland. John Owen was commanded to accompany Cromwell, now as an adviser as well as chaplain. Having fought and won the Battle of Dunbar, the English troops stormed Edinburgh, and Cromwell put his preachers in the city's churches. John Owen took the services in St Giles.

'How dare Cromwell put one of his men in our pulpit!' an elder said, as he went into church the first Sunday.

'Thank goodness it's Mr Owen and not another of Cromwell's men,' he thought the following week.

And the next Sunday, as he took his seat in church, the elder found himself looking forward to what John Owen had to say. 'He may be Cromwell's chaplain,' he told his wife, as they walked home after the service, 'but he preaches about the Lord Jesus Christ and makes me want to listen.'

Oliver Cromwell had removed all the Roman Church practices from Oxford University, and he was so pleased with John Owen that he appointed him Vice-Chancellor and Dean of Christ Church. Cromwell was clever; he knew that the university had been nearly ruined, and that his friend would put it to rights again. And that's just what the new Vice-Chancellor helped to happen.

'What do you think of Mr Owen?' one student asked another, as they fished in the Thames one Saturday.

'He's a good man,' his friend answered. 'He doesn't only preach the Bible, he actually lives a good Christian life.'

'What makes you say that?' queried the student.

His friend re-cast, letting his cork float settle in the water before answering.

'My father died not long after I came to Oxford,' he said. 'And until my uncle sent me some money I had nothing at all to live on. Somehow Mr Owen heard about that, and he gave me enough to see me through.'

Although Owen's work kept him very busy, it didn't stop him writing. He wrote many books that were popular in his own day, and that are still read today. John didn't find it easy to say things in just a few words, so his books can be heavy reading. Someone has suggested that they are easier to understand when read aloud, because then it sounds as though John Owen is speaking.

In 1657, a majority of Members of Parliament voted to crown Cromwell as king.

'That's not right,' John thought. 'He is a good military ruler, but not a good king. I hope he has the sense to know that.'

But Cromwell thought differently, and he wasn't pleased with John. Owen and several others drew up a petition against Parliament's ruling, and Cromwell was forced to stand down. Instead, in a very grand ceremony, he was made Lord Protector. John was not even invited to the ceremony. Three years later, when Charles II was crowned king, Owen was forced to resign his job and leave Oxford. Although he was not legally allowed to preach, he continued to do so when he could. Of course, no law could stop him writing his books.

London went through terrible times in the mid-1660s. The Great Plague hit the city and at its height, in September 1665, more than 8000 people died each week. Then the Great Fire of London roared through the streets. While many ministers the king approved of fled the city in terror, John Owen and others who thought as he did (they were called Puritans) were soon back in London preaching the good news that Jesus saves.

Although John Owen was one of the cleverest men of his time, his friends were not all grand people. One of them, John Bunyan, was a tinker, who had spent time in prison for his faith.

'I hear you wrote a book in prison. What's it about?' Owen asked his friend.

'It's a story, a kind of fantasy, about the Christian life,' Bunyan explained.

'May I read it?' enquired John.

Bunyan gave 'The Pilgrim's Progress' to his friend, and John Owen was so impressed by it that he asked his publisher to produce the book. That was a wise decision as 'The Pilgrim's Progress' is probably the best-known Christian book of all time. John Owen knew that God could use tinkers as well as professors to teach people about the Lord Jesus Christ.

Fact File: *Pilgrim Fathers.*
John Owen was a Puritan, and there were times when the government made life very difficult for Puritans. In 1620, some of them decided to set sail for America in a ship called 'The Mayflower'. They landed on the coast of Massachusetts and settled in a place that they called Plymouth.

The voyage and the first winter were very difficult, and half of those who set out on the voyage had died by the spring of 1621. However, none of them wanted to return to England. Their condition improved as time went on. There are still people in America descended from these 'Pilgrim Fathers'.

Keynote: Although Cromwell was a brave and successful soldier, John Owen wasn't afraid to tell him when he thought that he was making a mistake. It is important to get on with our friends, but we need to remember that true friends are ready to give and take correction when they do something wrong.

We need to be careful, however, that we give correction in the right way. Even when we do this, as John did, our friends might be upset. But it is important to tell them the truth all the same. It is also important to accept correction in the right way. If someone points out to you that you have made a mistake, or are doing something wrong, you should thank them for telling you.

 Think: The teaching that John received from his father and from Mr Sylvester helped him to do great things for God later in life. John benefited from going to Oxford as his father told him he would, even though he did not want to go at first. Think about times when you have been told to do things that you didn't want to do, but which later proved to be good for you. Remember these, and John's example, the next time that it's sunny outside but there is a room to tidy inside, or other work to do.

 Prayer: Thank you, Lord Jesus, for those who teach me, and especially for those who teach me about you. Please help me to listen to them carefully and to use what I learn in a way that pleases you. Please help children who do not have anyone to teach them about you. Amen.

Jonathan Edwards

Jonathan lay absolutely still on the grass, hardly daring to breathe. Just in front of him was what he had hoped to see. A tiny spider climbed up a twig on a low bush, then it stopped and seemed to rub all of its legs together. A moment later, it swung to another branch, and the boy could see just the faintest glint of sunshine on the very first strand of a web. He was fascinated. Quite unaware of the time, Jonathan lay there, watching the spider go back and forth and up and down, then round and round the web until the job was done. Even though he was stiff from lying still, he didn't move a muscle as the spider worked.

'How does the spider produce the threads that make the web?' he wondered. 'How does it manage to swing up through the air as well as down? And how do the strands of the web stick together?' Later, as he walked back to his home in New England, Jonathan tried to work it out. 'I think that when the spider was rubbing all its legs together, it was making some kind of juice flow, and that the juice doesn't dry immediately when the spider threads it between the branches. If it did dry immediately the web wouldn't stick together, every strand would dangle separately.'

'Where have you been?' one of Jonathan's cousins asked, when he arrived back home.

'I was spider-watching as usual,' replied the boy.

'Again!' his Stoughton cousins said together.

'May I come with you next time?' asked Jonathan's younger sister.

He looked at her, and doubted that she'd stay still enough to see anything.

'Yes,' he said. 'You can come with me first thing tomorrow morning before school. I saw a brilliant web being made today, and we'll see if it has caught anything by morning.'

His sister grinned.

'But you'll have to be quiet and still,' he warned her.

Early the following morning, Jonathan and his sister went back to the spider's bush. There had been a heavy dew and the sun was just beginning to shine.

'Shh,' he told his little sister. 'Follow me and don't make a noise.'

At first she couldn't see the web at all. But when her brother pointed to it, she thought she'd never seen anything more beautiful in her life. Dew hung from the strands of the web like diamond drops, each one reflecting the light of the morning sun.

'Where's the spider?' the girl asked.

'I don't know, Jonathan replied. 'But we'll see her if we come back later when the web has had time to dry out.'

As they walked back home, Jonathan's mind was busy.

'Water is heavy,' he thought. 'I wonder what the weight of all the dewdrops on the web would be. It must be very strong not to break under their weight.'

'We'll have to hurry or we'll be late for school,' the girl said, as they walked through the wood.

The pair of them broke into a run, and arrived back just on time.

Having dashed into the kitchen to wash their hands, Jonathan and his sister arrived in the schoolroom red-faced and breathless. Their father, who was also their teacher, smiled. 'I hear you've been spider-watching,' he said, as they sat down on their benches.

School was held in a room in Jonathan's home. His father, Timothy Edwards, was a minister and schoolmaster. And the pupils were mainly family. There was Jonathan and his six sisters, their seven Stoughton cousins, and some boys from the village. After school that day, Mr Edwards went for a walk with his brother-in-law, Captain Thomas Stoughton.

'Thanks for showing me the essay Jonathan wrote about spiders,' Captain Thomas said. 'That boy has a remarkable mind.'

Mr Edwards nodded. 'He seems to be able to work things out for himself rather than just accepting what other people say.'

'I agree,' the Captain said. 'But it's more than that. He can also explain his thinking to other people.'

'There's something I want to ask you, Dad,' Jonathan said, after tea one evening.

Mr Edwards shook his head. 'You always have things you want to ask. I've never met another boy with so many whys in his brain.'

But as the man could see there was something troubling his son, he made sure they had time to talk. Jonathan didn't only want to understand spiders, he wanted to understand life. And he wanted to understand the Bible too, not just accept what his father taught and preached. That night they discussed some very difficult questions, and the boy's mind turned them over and over again as he tried to go to sleep.

'Is every word in the Bible true?' he asked himself. 'Is it really God's word speaking to us?'

He fluffed up his pillow to make himself more comfortable.

'And is Jesus actually God's son?'

When he awoke the following morning, even more questions had appeared in his mind than had been there the previous evening.

Before Jonathan left home for college in 1710, when he was thirteen-years-old, he realised for himself that what he had been taught was true, and he put his trust in the Lord Jesus as his Saviour. After that he thought of spider-watching as exploring the wonderful world of nature God made.

Yale College, where Jonathan studied for the ministry for four years, is now very famous, but then it was a new college, just two years older than Jonathan Edwards. During his studies there, the boy from New England had a difficult time. There were a great many arguments about what people believed, just as there are today. Jonathan's sharp mind helped him work out what the Bible really said. That did not make him

Yale's most popular student, even though he graduated with two degrees, one in 1720 and the other in 1723.

'I think you should accept the offer of working with Grandfather Stoddard,' Timothy Edwards told his son, four years later. 'And when he is no longer able to work, you'll most likely become the minister of his congregation in Northampton.'

The young man shook his head. 'I'm not sure,' he said, thinking of his grandfather, his mother's father. 'He's a fine old man, but I don't agree with all that he says.'

'But you could still work with him,' his father insisted. 'And Northampton would be a good place to begin family life with Sarah.'

Jonathan thought of his young wife, and prayed about what he should do. Eventually he decided that going to Northampton was the right thing to do. Two years later, Grandfather Stoddard died, and Jonathan took over his big congregation.

'Tell me how you spend your days,' a visitor asked Jonathan Edwards, after he had been in Northampton for some years.

'I get up at 4am,' Jonathan said, 'and I reckon to spend 13 hours a day studying. In the afternoons I take some exercise by chopping wood, fencing or whatever else needs to be done. And if the weather is good, I often ride out to a place where I get peace to study. After tea I spend an hour with Sarah and the children, before taking my candle and getting back to work again.'

'How many children do you have now?' his friend asked.

Jonathan smiled as he thought of his young family. 'We have five, and another on the way.'

Eventually John and Sarah had eleven children, eight girls and three boys.

Jonathan's ministry was not always easy, because he disagreed with some of the things his grandfather had taught. But in 1734, the town of Northampton was buzzing with news of what was happening in the church.

'Did you hear that a young rogue was converted? Last week he was cursing his way down the street, this week he's singing hymns!' one neighbour said to another.

'And Abigail Hutchinson too, though she's a frail young thing, has changed completely! She's so full of joy,' her friend replied.

A man coming along the road heard what the two women were saying.

'The most remarkable conversion story I heard was about Phebe Bartlette.'

'Phebe?' one of the women said. 'But she's just a baby.'

'Not quite a baby,' corrected the man. 'She's four years old, and she's become a Christian.'

The two women walked a little further along the road.

'Is that Mr Baker?' one asked, puzzled at the sight.

The man heard his name and smiled.

'It is indeed,' he said, 'though you've never seen me sober before. But I'm a Christian now, and I've given up the drink for better things.'

The taller of the two women nudged her friend. 'Cross the road,' she whispered, out of the corner of her mouth. 'Greta the Gossip's coming our way.'

But before they could cross, Greta was right beside them.

'I want to apologise for all those years of gossiping,' the old woman said. 'I've been a nasty bit of work, but from now on you'll not hear another word of gossip from me. And if you do, please tell me to stop talking about people and talk about Jesus.'

Before the two women could think of what to say, Greta had spotted someone else she wanted to apologise to, and was off.

For months the news was about people becoming Christians. News spread, and visitors began to go to Northampton to see for themselves what was happening there.

Many went home changed, and the things that happened in Jonathan's church began to happen in many other places too. 1734 to 1736 were exciting times for the Edwardses. And in 1740, when Jonathan invited the famous preacher, George Whitefield, to preach in Northampton, the same wonderful things began all over again.

Ten years later, Jonathan and Sarah sat on either side of the fire in their little living room. It was dark, and the candle was nearly done. All the children who were still at home were sound asleep in bed.

'Just a decade ago,' Jonathan said, 'people were being converted, the church was growing, and it would have been full if we'd had a service every night of the week.'

Sarah smiled. 'I remember it well,' she said. 'Those were the good days.'

'And today the congregation voted for me to leave Northampton,' added her husband sadly. 'I'm not surprised though, it's been coming for some time.'

'You did the right thing,' Sarah assured Jonathan. 'Because what Grandfather Stoddard taught was sometimes a little different from the Bible, you had no choice but to tell the people the truth. Your father once told me that you'd been like that since you were a little boy. You worked things out carefully in your mind, then explained your thinking to other people.'

Jonathan smiled for the first time that day.

'I used to watch spiders for hours,' he said. 'Then I worked out how they made their webs and explained it to the others at school. I imagine that's what he was thinking about.'

'It was indeed,' laughed Sarah. 'He told me about the spiders!'

It was some months before Jonathan got another job, and when he did it was in a very spidery place! He became minister to the River Indians or Housatonics in the remote small town of Stockbridge, about 60 miles from Northampton. He also worked with the Mohawks and Iroquois. Jonathan Edwards wrote many books while he was at Northampton and he continued to write in Stockbridge. He was quite famous by this time, and visitors came all the way to his new home to talk with him.

'Is this where you write your books?' one asked, as they sat in the living-room.

'No,' said Jonathan, 'there are still too many children at home to have peace to write in the living-room!'

'May I see your study?' enquired the visitor, a little cheekily.

The minister smiled. 'Only if you are short-sighted,' he joked, 'because the walls will be very near your nose in all four directions. 'Come and see for yourself.'

Jonathan opened the door to his study. 'Don't get lost,' he laughed.

His guest went through the door into what looked just like a cupboard. The study the famous author wrote in was just seven feet long and three-and-a-half feet wide!

'You'll certainly get peace in there,' the man said. 'There's no room for company.'

'That's where you're wrong,' Edwards told him. 'If you look up to the ceiling corners, you'll discover that I have the company of some rather fine spiders!'

Jonathan studied the Indians' language, though his children learned it much more quickly than he did. For seven years he worked among the Housatonics and other Indian peoples, and many of them became Christians. He also helped to keep the peace when war threatened the area around Stockbridge. At the end of 1752, he was asked to become Principal of the college that is now the famous Princeton Theological Seminary. Just three months after moving there, before Sarah was able to join him, Jonathan Edwards fell ill and died. Amazingly, some of the books he wrote in the 1700s have never been out of print since the day they were first published!

Fact File: *Spiders.*
Jonathan watched spiders very carefully and was very interested in how they spun their webs. Spiders' webs are made of silk which comes out of glands in the spider. The silk becomes sticky when it comes into contact with the air. Spiders use their silk for many purposes – even making threads to swing on – but the most common use is to make webs to catch insects.

The silk is very strong and stretchy. As well as the many uses that spiders have for it, some telescope manufacturers use it to make the cross-hairs on their telescopes.

Keynote: Jonathan realised the importance of studying the Bible closely, and really looking to see what it has to say. When he was preaching to people, he was careful to stick closely to the Bible. It is still important that we stick to the Bible when we are trying to learn about God. We need to know it well in order to do that.

Remember Jonathan's enthusiasm for studying the Bible as you hear it read and explained, and as you read it yourself.

Think: When Jonathan had questions about parts of the Bible that he did not understand, he asked his father about them. He realised that he could not work it all out for himself. We can all learn from others when we are trying to understand the Bible. Think about people you could go to with questions about the Bible, and think carefully about what you learn in the Bible, just as Jonathan did.

Prayer: Lord Jesus, thank you for all of the amazing things that you have created. Thank you for spiders, birds, insects and animals. Thank you for your word, the Bible and for all that it has to teach us about you. Please help me to study it carefully so that I can know you better and love you more. Thank you for those who can explain the Bible to me. Amen.

George Whitefield

Mrs Whitefield looked at her four-year-old son and wondered if he would survive the night. His body was covered with measles spots, and his face was red with fever. She washed him gently to try to bring his temperature down, but all night the fever raged.

'Is George going to die?' an older brother asked.

His mother shook her head. 'Don't say such a thing. Go and pray that he'll get better.'

But in her heart she nearly despaired of her little son. The following day things were no better, and a woman came to help with nursing the lad.

'You have six others to think about,' she told Mrs Whitefield. 'You see to them and I'll do what I can for this poor mite.'

George struggled to speak, and the nurse bent toward him to hear what he was saying.

'He wants water,' she announced to the child's sister. 'Get me a cup of water for the boy.'

Mrs Whitefield did what she was told. She had been up all night and was too tired to argue. All day she was busy with her six older children, all boys apart from one girl. Every time she had a minute she ran through to see if George was still alive.

'Is it my imagination?' she wondered, as the afternoon wore on, 'or is his fever going down at last?'

By evening it was clear that the boy was a little better, and the following morning proved it.

'I want a drink!' George announced crossly from his bed. 'I'm thirsty and I want a drink!'

His mother nearly wept with joy that her youngest son would live. But something was different about him, and she couldn't quite work it out.

'George's eyes are funny,' his sister said, a week or two later. 'They don't both look in the same direction.'

While the boy recovered from measles, he was left with a squint in his eye. And because he had such very dark eyes, everyone noticed the squint.

Two or three years later, young George was out playing with his friends when a stranger approached them on horseback.

'Let's be highwaymen and ambush him,' the boy suggested. 'Run up the lane and get handfuls of stones.'

George was very much the leader of the gang, and his friends did exactly what they were told.

'Your money or your life!' George Whitefield yelled, as they pelted the stranger with small stones.

The man reined his horse to a standstill.

'Cheeky scoundrels!' said the rider, sliding off his horse in a flash.

Before George knew what was happening to him, he was being held very firmly by the ear.

'Take me to your father,' the man demanded.

'I don't have one,' George mumbled.

This was too much for the angry man. 'What do you mean you don't have one? Everybody has a father!'

'Please sir,' one of the other boys said, 'George's father died when he was a baby and he can't remember him.'

The stranger was kinder than the boys deserved. Feeling sorry for the fatherless boy, he told them to behave themselves in future or they would come to a bad end, then he mounted his horse and rode on.

But George didn't take the man's advice, and he didn't get any better. His dares went from bad to worse, and he was so often in trouble that his mother nearly despaired of him. Even though she loved him dearly, he even stole from her purse when he wanted to play cards for money. And he wasn't just a pest at home, he was known in the town as a troublemaker.

'I dare you to do the Meeting-house!' one of George's friends said, on a Sunday when they should have been at church but were not.

George knew exactly what 'doing the Meeting-house' meant, and it sounded fun.

'Come on, you lot!' he said, 'and see if I can shout louder than old man Cole.'

They ran along the streets till they came to the Meeting-house where Mr Cole was preaching his sermon.

George strode in, walked up the aisle, and shouted at the top of his voice, 'Old Cole! Old Cole! Old Cole!'

The minister tried to preach through the noise, but George out-shouted him, and he had to stop. The old man bowed his head and prayed for the lad. Thinking that he had won the shouting match, George lost interest in the game and left the Meeting-house to look for some other mischief to get up to.

Seven years later, in 1732, he was a very different George Whitefield. His mother married again, but not very happily. And although he had left school at 15, he was now about to become a student at Oxford University. Because he was poor, he had also to work as a servant there. Within a year he became a member of the Holy Club, where he met Christians who had a great influence on him. Two of them, John and Charles Wesley, became very famous preachers. It was in Oxford, in 1735, that George took all his sins to Jesus, even his stone-throwing and his disrupting the Meeting-house services, and he asked the Lord to forgive him. God answered his prayer, and George began a new life as a Christian. Less than four years later he was a minister.

Returning to London, George thought he would be able to preach in some of the city's churches. But because he was friends with the Wesley brothers, who were not Church of England, many churches would not have George in their pulpits!

'I hear there is a Welshman who preaches to crowds in the open air,' Whitefield told the Wesleys. 'Do you think I should be doing that too?'

Soon afterwards, George preached at his first open-air meeting. Despite it being a cold February day, over 200 people came to listen. Before long the crowds coming to hear the new preacher had grown to upwards of 35,000, and their singing could be heard two miles away!

'What a mess you're in,' a friend said, seeing George immediately after he had preached to a huge crowd at Moorfields, near London.

His friend grinned. 'I was honoured with having stones, dirt, rotten eggs and pieces of dead cat thrown at me.'

'Doesn't sound much of an honour,' his friend commented. 'I thought everyone who went to an open-air service would be above that sort of thing.'

Shaking his head, George assured his companion that he was wrong there, and that some people just went to make mischief. Deep in his heart, he knew that if open-airs had taken place in Gloucester when he was a boy, he would have been right in the thick of it making all the mischief he could.

As they walked along the road, his friend questioned him further about what happened at his open-airs.

George grinned. 'You know some people say I should have been an actor rather than a preacher?'

The other man said he thought that might be a good idea!

'You may be right!' the preacher laughed.

'One day I was preaching about Jesus calming the storm at sea. I painted as vivid a picture as I possibly could, so much so I could almost feel the salt spray in my face. And I obviously wasn't the only one who got carried away, because just as I reached the climax of the sermon an old sailor in the crowd jumped to his feet and yelled, "To the lifeboats, men! To the lifeboats!"'

Whitefield's friend laughed heartily, and said that perhaps he should have been an actor after all!

On 1st August 1739, the Bishop of London denounced the young preacher, and banned him from every Church of England building. Two weeks later, George was on his way to America. The Wesleys were already there, and they wrote asking him to join them. He had been there for a time in the previous year, and had established an orphanage and school for poor children. By the time he returned a year later, he had collected a large amount of money for the orphans.

'Why do you bother yourself with these fatherless children?' an American woman asked him one day.

George stopped what he was doing, and looked her in the eye. 'I was a poor fatherless child myself,' he said. 'I ran wild, and could have become the worst rogue in

Gloucester. If God had not saved me, I'd not be here in America preaching the gospel, I'd be back in England in a dark prison cell.'

Very embarrassed, the lady rifled about in her bag and found some money to go towards the orphanage.

'Thank you, Ma'am,' said George. 'And who knows, perhaps God will raise some preachers from among these dear orphan lads.'

In March 1740, the foundation stone was laid of Bethesda, the main part of his orphan home in Savanah.

George Whitefield led a travelling life. He had no settled church, and he preached where he was invited. In a day when travelling was not easy, and journeys could take many months, he travelled the length and breadth of England, as well as Scotland, Ireland, Wales, Gibraltar, Bermuda and America.

'What was your biggest open-air?' he was asked one day.

'I couldn't begin to guess,' he replied, 'but I suppose over 40,000.'

'And your smallest?'

George smiled. 'I remember the smallest one well. I was on my way across the Atlantic, and the ship we were on was so buffeted by a storm that the sails were tattered and the gear was a mess. My pulpit was the swaying deck, and the congregation was just 30 people, some looking more seasick than others. I remember on that voyage my blanket was a buffalo hide and, although my quarters were in the driest part of the vessel, there were nights when I was drenched through more than once.'

'I don't know why you go back and forward across the Atlantic,' his friend said, after hearing that story.

'I do,' Whitefield replied. 'I go because people ask me to preach the good news of Jesus. But there's another reason besides that.'

'Oh,' said the other man, 'what's that?'

George's eyes grew soft as he thought of Savanah. 'My wife and I only had one child, a boy, and he died. But I have a home in Savanah that's full of orphan children I think of as my own. Many of them never knew their fathers, as I never knew mine. And I'd happily cross the Atlantic Ocean to see the smiles on their faces when I arrive.'

'I suppose it is worth endangering your life then,' his companion said, although he was not quite convinced.

It was in Ireland, not in a storm at sea, that George Whitefield nearly lost his life. In 1756, he was preaching on a green near

Dublin, when a mob among the people who wanted to listen, started to throw clods of earth and stones at the preacher. When the crowd dispersed, the mob grew and threatened to take his life. He had a half-mile walk to safety, and all the time he was pelted with stones from every direction. A riot was soon in full swing, and blood poured from George's head as he tried to get away. Eventually he staggered to a minister's door and the murderous mob disappeared. The minister found an almost unconscious Whitefield on his doorstep. Lifting him to his feet, he helped him into the house and looked after him.

'Now I know what the Lord's apostles felt like when they were stoned by angry crowds,' he told his friend, when he felt a bit better.

George continued his travelling ministry, preaching to bigger and bigger crowds on both sides of the Atlantic Ocean, until he left for America for the last time in September 1769. He went to upgrade his orphanage to Bethesda College, and he was especially looking forward to seeing some English people there. Whitefield had taken 22 orphans to America 15 years before, and he was interested to see what kind of young men they had grown into. Having spent the winter at Bethesda, he travelled north to preach. Huge numbers of people gathered to hear him, and he preached his heart out.

A year after arriving in America, while he was staying with a friend, a large company came to the house to meet him. They talked until late at night. George, who was ill and tired, said goodnight and was about to go to bed when one of the visitors asked him to give them just a short talk. By then Whitefield was actually on the stairs with a candle in his hand! He turned round and preached until the candle went out then climbed the stairs wearily and went to bed. George had preached his very last sermon, and he died without ever getting out of bed again. But that was not the end of the man, his work went on at Bethesda, and many of those who had heard him preach became preachers themselves, and continued to tell people the good news that Jesus Christ is the Saviour of all who trust in him, even rogues and rascals like the young George Whitefield.

Fact File: *Transatlantic Travel.* It was very dangerous for George Whitefield to cross the Atlantic in a ship, but at that time it was the only way to get to America from Europe. Not many people made the trip. Even 100 years after Whitefield, many people who left Britain to go to America knew that they would never come back to their homes. Today, however, it is much easier to travel between Europe and America. An aeroplane can complete the journey in less than eight hours, and Concorde can do it in three-and-a-half hours.

 Keynote: George travelled all over the world, sometimes taking great risks so that he could preach about Jesus. This is not the behaviour that might have been expected from the boy who shouted down the preacher in the Meeting-house. God is able to change all sorts of people and make them into his servants.

In the book of Acts we read about a man called Saul who was very angry with Christians and did lots of bad things to them. But God spoke to him and turned him into one of the greatest missionaries ever.

Think: As well as preaching, George took care of many orphans. He did this because God had taken care of him although he was fatherless.

Think about some of the good things that God has done for you. How can you follow George's example by showing thankfulness and helping others? Remember that God loves us and invites us to come to him as children to their father.

Prayer: Lord God, thank you for being so good and kind to us. Thank you for inviting us to call you 'Father'. Please help us to love you as we should, and to try our best to help others. Please watch over all the children whose mums and dads have died, and help them to know you as their heavenly Father. Amen.

Robert Murray McCheyne

'It's snowing!' Robert yelled, as he looked out of the window. 'Look, the hills are white!'

'We have a great view from this part of Edinburgh,' his older brother David said. 'Although we live just a few minutes' walk from the centre of the city, from here we can see right over the Firth of Forth to the snowy hills of Fife.'

'But we won't be able to see them for long,' Robert laughed. 'The snow's getting heavier. Look at the size of the snowflakes!'

'You'll be wanting to go sledging before long,' said David.

Robert's love for anything sporty was almost a family joke.

'If there's a tree, Robert will swing from it,' Mr McCheyne often commented. 'If there's a hill he'll be the first to climb it, and whenever he sees water he wants to be in for a swim. There's just no stopping the boy!'

By the end of that afternoon Robert's sledge was covered in snow, and so was he.

Despite a bath when he came in, and a rub-down with a warm towel, the following day the boy was in bed with a chill.

'I worry about Robert,' David told his father. 'He's so often ill.'

'I know,' Mr McCheyne agreed. 'But he bounces up again, and before long he's running about all over the place.'

'How are you feeling?' asked David, sitting down on his brother's bed.

Robert, who was still shivery, ignored the question and pointed to a picture in the book he was reading.

'Look at this,' he said. 'Did you know that ants can carry leaves much bigger than themselves, even leaves that weigh much more than they do?'

David admitted that was news to him. Then he burst out laughing.

'What's so funny?' Robert asked.

'I was just remembering back five years. You were four years old and in bed unwell. We were looking for something to interest you so we taught you the Greek alphabet. In just one week you learned to read and write all the letters.'

'And I still remember them,' the boy said. 'Alpha, beta, gamma, delta ..'

'OK,' his brother laughed. 'I believe you.'

When David took a cup of hot milk to his brother a short time later, Robert was told to sit up and listen.

'I've written a poem for you,' David said.

'A boy was in bed with a bug,
all warmly wrapped in a rug.
His brothers were doing their best
to keep him in bed for a rest.
They taught him alpha and beta
and because he wasn't a cheater
he learned the letters well,
and that's why he can tell
that bed is the best place to be
if you want some time to be free
to study in peace and quiet.'

Robert smiled. 'That's great!' he said. 'But the last line doesn't rhyme with anything.'

'Well, I had to get you this milk! I can't do everything you know.' David told him.

Although Robert was often off school because of illness, he worked very hard and did well in his studies. And he was not only noticed because he worked hard.

'I remember McCheyne as a tall thin lad with a pleasant face,' a friend wrote many years later. 'He was bright and serious yet fond of play and he lived a good life. I especially remember his tartan trousers, which I both admired and envied.'

'Will you come on a walking holiday?' Robert asked his friend Malcolm, when they were teenagers.

Malcolm agreed, and they planned to explore the countryside around Dunkeld in Perthshire. All went well until they crossed the hills to Strathardle and a mist came down.

'I can't see where we're going,' Robert said, as the mist turned into fog that seemed to grow thicker by the minute.

'Let's keep going downhill and we'll maybe get below the fog level,' suggested Malcolm.

The boys slithered and skidded down the hillside, but the fog had reached the valley too.

'I can hear running water,' Robert said. 'If we find the river and follow it, we'll reach safety.'

'I don't think we should do that,' Malcolm decided. 'It's not only foggy, it's dark now. If you fell and broke your leg and I went for help, I'd never be able to find you again. I think we should bed down in the bracken and try to get some sleep.'

'Travelling adventures are fine when everything goes well,' Robert thought, as they tried to get to sleep. 'But it's not so good when things go wrong.'

The next morning dawned bright and sunny, and the two boys woke to the sound of moorcock, grouse and loudly rumbling stomachs!

When Robert Murray McCheyne was just 14, he became a student at Edinburgh University. Four years later, in 1831, the bottom fell out of his world. His brother David became ill and it was soon clear that he would not get better. David was a Christian, and his love of the Lord Jesus made a deep impression on his younger brother. When David died, Robert's heart broke. Much later he wrote to a friend, 'This day eleven years ago I lost my loved and loving brother, and began to seek a Brother who cannot die.' So it was through David's death that Robert began to search for Jesus, the friend whom the Bible says, sticks closer than a brother. And like all who seek Jesus, Robert found him as his Saviour, Brother and Friend. When Robert graduated from university in 1835, all he wanted to do was to introduce others to Jesus. After a short time assisting a minister in central Scotland, Robert became minister of St Peter's Church in Dundee. Soon his church was full of people every Sunday. They came from around the church and from other parts of Dundee as well.

'Why do you think so many people have started going to hear the new minister at St Peter's?' asked a man who lived near the church, but who never went inside it.

One of Robert's elders was passing at the time, and answered the man's question.

'Mr McCheyne loves the Lord Jesus with all his heart, and his preaching is just full of that love.'

The man snorted. 'At least that's different from all the others who preach about hell's fire every Sunday.'

'How do you know what other ministers preach when you're never inside a church?' the elder asked.

Winking and tapping his ear, the man answered, 'I hear as much by hanging around outside a church as most people hear who go in to the service.'

Speaking gently and seriously to the old man, the elder said, 'Then you'll no doubt have heard that when Mr McCheyne mentions hell in his sermons the tears often run down his cheeks at the thought of anyone going there.'

'I have 170 girls and 70 young men in my Bible Class,' Robert wrote to his brother William, six months after moving to Dundee. 'I use what I call the Geographical Method of teaching. I give them out some place, such as the Sea of Galilee, and get them to look up where it is mentioned in the Bible. Then I draw a map, as we used to do at school. I also read passages about the place from history books and from modern travellers. I find this interesting and they seem quite delighted with it. You'll find my map of the Sea of Galilee in with this letter, and you mustn't smile at my map-making!'

Perhaps one of the reasons why Robert liked teaching young people was that he was still young himself. And his father would not have been surprised to know that he continued to enjoy gymnastics even after he was a minister.

On one occasion he came a cropper. Robert's sister, Eliza, who lived with him, must have been worried when her brother was brought home cut and bruised.

'It happened when he was visiting his friend,' she told a neighbour. 'Apparently Robert put up some gymnastic poles in the garden and challenged his friend's son to a trial of skill.'

'The boy must have been delighted with that,' the neighbour smiled.

Eliza nodded her head. 'I'm sure he was!'

Amused at the idea of her minister doing gymnastics, the neighbour waited to hear what happened next.

'Robert went first to show the boy what to do,' explained Eliza, 'He was hanging by his heels and hands six feet above the ground when the poles snapped and he landed with a tremendous thud.'

The neighbour, suddenly realising that things might have been serious, was concerned.

'He was winded, cut and bruised,' Eliza concluded. 'God was good to him. He might have been killed.'

On that occasion Robert had to rest for some days because of his injuries, but other times he had to take to his bed because he was ill. Although he was athletic and really enjoyed exercise, he was never strong. His hard work wore him down, and more than once Eliza was very worried in case he would not recover. But as soon as Robert was fit to be up and dressed, he was always back to work.

In 1839, Robert Murray McCheyne was asked to go with a small group of others on a fact-finding trip to the Holy Land. It was the first time any ministers of the Church of Scotland had done such a thing.

'Are you well enough for such a long journey?' Eliza worried.

Her brother's eyes shone with excitement. 'If God wants me to go,' he said, 'he'll give me the health and strength I need.' His face broke into a wide smile. 'Eliza,' he said, 'I just can't believe that I'll walk where Jesus walked, and see the Sea of Galilee, the Mount of Olives, and other places the Lord saw when he was alive on earth!'

Realising that there was no possibility of persuading her brother to back out of the trip, Eliza set about getting his clothes prepared, and buying medicines for him to take with him just in case.

The places the little group of ministers visited reads like a travel brochure. Robert's diary records their journey by sea to London, then across the English Channel to France before travelling overland to Italy, Valetta, Alexandria and eventually the Holy Land. Having left Dundee in March, they reached Jerusalem in June. Robert wrote to tell his mother about it.

'This is one of the most privileged days of my life,' he wrote. 'I left my camel and hurried over the burning rocks. In about half an hour Jerusalem came into sight!'

For more than a week the men camped at the foot of Mount Carmel, and explored the area, paying special attention to the Jewish people they met on their travels. They were introduced to a Jewish Christian who was able to give them a vast amount of information. The man was delighted to learn that the Church in Scotland had sent ministers all the way to the Holy Land to find out the best way to tell Jewish people about Jesus the Messiah.

Although at one point on the journey Robert became so ill that his companions thought he would die, he recovered enough on the way home to be able to visit many Jewish areas of Eastern Europe. They even went as guests to a Jewish wedding. Knowing that his sister would be interested, be drew a picture of the bride's dress and sent it to her! The wedding was much more pleasant than another incident Robert described.

'Two evil-minded shepherds made signs that I should follow them,' he wrote. 'When I refused, things became quite ugly. I could have run away, but I knew my heart wouldn't stand it. I raised my stick, but I didn't want to hit out at them. Eventually I sat down. That confused them and they went away!'

Nine months after leaving, the travellers returned home, and the information they brought with them was used to plan how to reach Jewish people with the good news that the Messiah they were waiting for had come, and that his name was Jesus.

When Robert returned to Dundee, he discovered that God had done a wonderful work in his congregation while he was away. Many people, adults and children, had become Christians.

'Doesn't your brother mind that it was when another minister was preaching that this all happened?' someone asked his sister.

Eliza shook her head. 'He is just delighted to see his dear people trust in Jesus.'

For nearly three years, Robert looked after his congregation in Dundee and thrilled each time someone became a Christian. It was a special delight to him when children and young people trusted in Jesus, because they would have their whole lives to live in his service.

In 1842, when Robert was 29 years old, he became ill once again, but this time he did not recover. He had never been strong, and he had worn himself out. After he died, a letter arrived for him. It was from someone who had heard him preach just the previous week. The letter read, 'I heard you preach last Sunday and God blessed what you said to my heart. But it wasn't just what you said that meant so much to me, it was how you said it. I saw in you a beauty of holiness that I've never seen in anyone before.'

By the time that letter arrived, Robert Murray McCheyne was enjoying all the beauty of his Saviour in heaven.

Fact File: *Dundee.*
Robert was a minister in Dundee and he went to the Holy Land. But he wasn't the only person from Dundee to travel far and wide. In the past, Dundee was a thriving port that traded with other cities in Northern Europe and beyond. It was best known for trading in jute, which is used to make sacks. Another citizen of Dundee who is well-known is Mary Slessor. She went out as a missionary to Calibar in Africa in the 19th century. You can read about her in Ten Girls Who Changed the World.

Keynote: Although Robert was very young when he died, God used him to make a great impact on many people. (His sermons are still being read today.) He suffered from illness a lot when he was a minister but he trusted God, even for the strength to make the difficult journey to the Holy Land. God has promised to make us strong in him, even when we are weak. We can see that he fulfilled that promise in McCheyne's life and he can do so in yours too.

Think: Two shepherds threatened Robert. He knew that his heart was too weak to let him run away. He did not want to hit them with his stick. When he sat down, however, they ran away. Think about how you can respond to threats in the same way: by trying to avoid a fight rather than win one. Do you think that Robert's example only applies when people are going to hit you?

Prayer: Lord Jesus, thank you for the health and strength that you have given me. Help me to use it to serve you, and to trust you to give me the strength to be the kind of person that you want me to be. Please watch over those who are ill, and help them to remember that you love them. Amen.

Dwight L. Moody

The Moody brothers rushed round the little farmstead at Northfield, hiding anything of value they could find.

'Put Dad's tools in the bushes!' one shouted.

Another ran for the cowshed. 'I'll take the new calf into the woods and tether it to a tree.'

Dwight, who was just four years old, was given some small things to hide among his wooden bricks.

'Don't tell anyone they are there,' he was warned.

The boy hadn't a clue what was going on, but he felt important at being given something special to do.

There was the rumble of a cart coming along the track.

'Now, don't any of you be saying a word,' Mrs Moody instructed her children. 'I'll do all the talking.'

A horse and cart drew up in front of the little house.

'You know what I've come for,' the visitor said, as he jumped down from the cart.

'I know very well,' agreed Mrs Moody, 'but I can't believe you've the heart to take away my husband's horse and buggy, and his cows as well, when he's only been dead four days.'

The man avoided looking Mrs Moody in the eye.

'I've come for the furniture too,' he said.

The woman's eyes filled with tears, but she was absolutely determined that he wouldn't see them. Picking up Dwight, she turned towards the house and strode in.

'I suppose I should be grateful that the law of Massachusetts prevents you taking the house as well,' she called, without turning around.

Striding into the house and lifting two chairs at once, the man turned and looked at the widow.

'I suppose you should,' he said, and continued on his business.

The Moody children watched later that afternoon, as the cart began to move, piled high with their belongings.

'I'll be back for the horse and buggy,' the man shouted as he left.

Mrs Moody gathered her children around her.

I kept the things safe among my bricks,' Dwight said.

His mother hugged him.

'So you did,' she agreed. 'And we still have your father's tools and a calf. We'll win through yet. You see if we don't.'

One month later there were two more Moody children to care for. That's when the twins were born. They never knew their dad.

In 1843, two years after his father died, Dwight had work to do as some of his older brothers had already left home.

'I'm glad we kept you,' the boy told his favourite cow. She was the one that had been hidden in the woods. 'And now you've given us a fine calf as well as gallons of milk to drink. Mum says your milk makes the finest butter and cheese in the state.'

Mrs Moody had been able to get one or two more cows in the time since her husband died, and Dwight's job was to look after them.

'Let's go,' the boy told the beasts. 'If you're wanting some new green grass you're going to have to walk to it.'

Striding out in front of them, and leading the way, Dwight headed for the meadow. When the cows stopped for a drink, he climbed on to a rugged fence to wait for them. Taking a long blade of grass between his thumbs, the boy tried to see how loud he could whistle. Suddenly the fence gave way under him and he clattered to the ground. The nearest fence post dislodged, fell on top of him, and pinned him down.

'Help!' the lad shouted, when he got his breath back. 'Help!'

But even as he shouted he knew there was nobody near enough to hear him. Trying as hard as he possibly could he pushed against the fencepost, but he couldn't make it move at all. The problem was leverage. His heavy boots were caught among the bars and he couldn't loosen his legs to help him lever the post off his back. Dwight was desperate.

'God,' he yelled, 'help me lift these heavy rails.'

As soon as he had prayed that prayer, he was able to get himself free. For a while after that he often prayed, but somehow he got out of the habit.

Eleven years later, by which time Dwight had decided that religion was boring and only for old folk, he set out by train for the city of Boston.

'I'll miss Mum,' he thought, as the train rattled along, 'but I won't miss working on the farm. I'll make her proud of me. One day I'll go home with enough money in my pockets to give her an easy life. Dwight L. Moody will make his name in Boston.'

Suddenly Dwight broke into a broad smile as he remembered that the name he'd been given at birth was Dwight Lyman Ryther Moody. Ryther was the name of Northfield's doctor. But when the doctor didn't give baby Dwight the gift of a sheep (that was the custom when a baby was called after someone) Ryther was dropped from his name!

On arrival in Boston, Dwight headed for a shoe shop his uncle owned and asked for a job.

'If you work for me you'll do it on my conditions,' his uncle told him, when he eventually agreed to take his nephew on. 'And one of these conditions is that you go to church and Sunday school every week.'

'No problem!' the lad said, trying to hide his amusement and irritation. 'You'll find I'm a hard worker,' he added, being much more interested in earning money than religion.

To Dwight's surprise he didn't find church as boring as he'd expected. He began to wonder if there might be something in the Christian faith after all. Over the months the thought bothered him when he wasn't busy working or enjoying himself.

In 1855, a year after he'd arrived in Boston, special services were held in his church. Dwight's Sunday school teacher decided to speak to all his pupils about the Lord. Arriving at the shoe shop to discover his pupil was in the back premises, he went though to see him. Putting his hand on Dwight's shoulder, he asked him to trust in Christ who loved him enough to die on the cross for him. Right there, in among piles of shoes, laces and boxes, the young man from Northfield put his faith in the Lord Jesus and became a Christian. He was nineteen years old. Before long he was on the move to Chicago. But although he was now a Christian, Dwight's main concern was still to make money.

'Why don't you go out into the alleys and streets to see what boys you can bring in?' asked the man in charge of the mission church Dwight attended.

That was a challenge, and Moody liked a challenge. Remembering how poor he had been as a child, Dwight was not embarrassed to be seen with the poor children of Chicago. When he arrived back at the mission, he had eighteen barefoot and ragged lads trailing behind him.

'Will you be back next week?' Moody asked his young friends after Sunday school.

'Only if you are,' the oldest one replied.

Dwight screwed up his face.

'I'll be here next time,' he assured them, then added, 'but my work often takes me away. You can come when I'm not here though.'

He knew from the looks on their faces that they would only attend Sunday school if he were there to bring them in.

It was 1858, and Dwight and a friend were deep in discussion.

'You think we should get what?' his friend asked in amazement.

Moody grinned. 'I think we should get an old railway truck and use it for our own mission Sunday school.'

Because he had a way with his friends, by the following Sunday the truck was theirs and an enthusiastic group of boys were desperate to explore it.

'In you come,' yelled Dwight over the noise. 'And bring your friends next time.'

They did, and before long the truck was bursting at the seams. A man Dwight knew heard about it, and gave him a building to replace it.

'I went to see the new Sunday school,' someone said, soon afterwards. 'There was no lighting in the house, and Moody had tried to light it with half-a-dozen candles. I found him with a candle in one hand, a Bible in the other, and a child on his knees that he was trying to teach. There were 25 to 30 there altogether, and they were as poor lads as you would find anywhere in Chicago.'

Before long girls started attending too. The number grew and grew, eventually becoming too big even for their new building, and they had to move again.

'How many do you have in your Sunday school?' Dwight was asked, when it was about two years old.

Moody grinned. 'It's hard to count when children swarm like bees, but the last estimate was 600!'

Eventually Dwight could not both hold down a job and do the children's work he loved so much. Giving up his work, he decided to live on his savings, believing that when his money ran out, God would provide him with all that he needed. 'And if that doesn't happen,' he told his friends, 'I'll take it as a sign that I've to go back to work.'

That didn't happen. From 1860 till the end of his life, Moody never had another paid job.

In November that year a very important visitor went to Chicago, Abraham Lincoln, the President-elect. He accepted an invitation to visit Dwight's school.

'I was once as poor as any boy in the school,' Lincoln told the children, 'but I am now President of the United States, and if you attend to what is taught you here, one of you may yet be President.'

Abraham Lincoln's visit came at a difficult time as the American Civil War was in full swing. Dwight thought, not altogether accurately, that most Southerners were slave-owners, and he was against slavery. He was also a pacifist; he didn't believe that fighting was the right way to settle a difference. But that didn't stop him wanting to help the soldiers who were fighting for the abolition of slavery. He was all for doing what he could for them.

In a letter to his brother he wrote about the work he was doing.

'I have some 500 or 800 people that are dependent on me for their daily food and new ones coming all of the time. I keep a saddled horse to ride around with to hunt up the poor people and then I have a man to wait on the folks as they come to my office. I have just raised money enough to erect a chapel for the soldiers at the camp 3 miles from the city. I hold a meeting down there every day and one in the city so you see I have 3 meetings to attend to every day beside calling on the sick. And that is not all. I have to go into the country about every week to buy wood and provisions for the poor, also coal, wheatmeal and corn.'

Although Dwight was incredibly busy, he still found time to fall in love. He and Emma were married in 1862, and they went on to have a family.

After the Civil War, Moody became very well-known as a preacher, and not just around the city of Chicago. He travelled as far as the United Kingdom, where huge crowds of people went to hear him. Eventually he teamed up with another American, Ira Sankey, who was a Christian singer and songwriter. When he sang, people were so moved that they often wept. The names Moody and Sankey were linked together, and they became as famous in the 1870s as television stars are today.

'Have you heard Mr Moody preaching?' people asked, on both sides of the Atlantic. 'His grammar is poor, but he can fairly pack a punch in his preaching.'

'And Mr Sankey's songs are so catchy I find myself singing them as I work,' others commented.

The duo visited city after city, and preached and sang to halls crowded with people. So popular were Sankey's hymns that they were printed and sold in millions. Had there been golden discs in the 1870s, Ira Sankey's walls would have been covered with them.

Although Dwight became famous, he was nowhere happier than back in Northfield, Massachusetts. Partly that was because it was home, but also because he had built two schools there, one for girls and the other for boys. He had never forgotten what it was like to be a poor lad, and he was always conscious of his own lack of education. Before he died, he also founded a college in Chicago to train Christian workers.

Dwight Moody was a great man but he wasn't perfect. Perhaps his children knew that better than anyone else. When he was grown up, one of his sons said that sometimes his father lost his temper with them. 'Then after we had gone up to bed, we would hear his heavy footsteps, and he'd come into our room and put a heavy hand on our heads and say, "I want you to forgive me, that wasn't the way Christ taught."' Only great men can ask their children to forgive them.

Fact File: *American Civil War.*
Moody had a visit from Abraham
Lincoln during the American Civil
War. This broke out in 1861, soon
after Lincoln was elected president.
There was a lot of disagreement
between the Northern and the
Southern states about how much
power the central government
should have and about slavery.

The war lasted until 1865, and
600,000 men were killed. The
Northern states won the war and
managed to prevent the Southern
states from breaking away and
forming their own 'Confederacy'.
Slavery was abolished shortly after
the end of the war.

 Keynote: Moody's love for little
children can be seen in the number
who attended the Sunday schools
that he was involved in.

Jesus loved children too, and
told his disciples to let the little
children come to him. This shows
us that we are never too young
to start learning about God, and

about all the amazing things that he has done for us. That was part of the reason that Moody was so enthusiastic about getting children to come to his Sunday school.

 Think: When Moody was a boy, he thought that religion was boring and didn't really want to go to Sunday school. But, when he did go to one in Boston, he found it more exciting than he had expected.

Think about the chances that you have to learn about God. Do you go to church and Sunday school expecting to learn new and exciting things every time? The children around Moody certainly seemed to do so.

 Prayer: Lord Jesus, thank you for those who teach me about you and all that you have done. Thank you for all the exciting things that there are to learn about in the Bible. Please help me to listen carefully, and to try and learn these things as well as I can. Amen.

Billy Sunday

The night was dark apart from the brightness of the sugaring fire, and young Billy Sunday was feeling good.

'I just love sugaring-off nights,' he told his grandfather.

The old man smiled. 'So do I, Son,' he said, 'especially as I built this old sugarcane mill myself.'

'It's very clever,' Billy said. 'I like watching the horse going round and round in a ring and working the mill that crushes the sugar cane until the sticky thick sap comes out. But best of all, I like when the sap is boiled and skimmed and we have to keep the fire going until all the sugaring-off is done.'

'You're a great help,' his grandfather said, 'especially when you feed the fire to keep the sap a-simmering. By this time of night, after a day on the mill, my poor old bones are aching so much I'm grateful for your help.'

'I've learned a lot from you,' Billy told the old man. 'You've taught me how to cut wood,

91

build fences, care for horses and milk the cows. And I can help with the crops too.'

Mr Sunday looked down at the eight-year-old. 'I had to teach you, Son,' he said, 'after your poor papa died just before you were born. Your mama couldn't teach you men's things.'

Billy swelled with pride at the thought of being a man.

'Tell me about my papa,' he asked, after a few minutes of staring into the firelight.

A sad look crossed his grandfather's face. 'It was in the summer of 1862, four months before you were born, that your father marched off to the sound of the fife and drum to be a soldier. And he never came back.'

'But he wasn't killed in a battle, was he?' queried the boy.

'No, he died of an illness before the battle had a chance to get him.'

'I would have liked to have a papa,' young Billy said.

Grandfather Sunday nodded. 'And I would like to have had a son. But you and your brothers have been sons to me, and I've been all the father you've ever had. And that's enough for now; the fire needs more wood and I'm too stiff to get up.'

Billy jumped to his feet and pushed fresh wood under the sugaring vat.

But two years later, Billy's life as a country boy came to a sudden end.

'Sons, I have something I've got to tell you,' Mrs Sunday said to Billy and his brother Edward one day.

The tone of her voice made the boys look at each other.

'I'm going to send the two of you to the Soldiers' Orphans Home at Glenwood. You've had all the schooling you can have here.'

'But how will we get there?' Edward asked. 'And how often will we get home?'

Edward, who was twelve, knew better than Billy what a huge change was about to happen in their lives.

It was 1 o'clock in the morning when the boys were put on a train at the local Ames station.

'Goodbye,' Edward said, hugging his tearful mother.

Then it was Billy's turn, and when he said, 'Goodbye,' he realised that he had never had to say goodbye to his mother before. She had always been there for him. When the train chugged out of Ames Station, the boys could not see their mother for the darkness. It was four long years before they saw her again; four long years before they had another long hug from their mother.

Living away from home and family was very hard but eventually there came a day when Edward and Billy finally returned home. However, things weren't easy then either as they both had to look for work.

Billy did a number of different jobs before going to work in Nevada for Colonel John Scott, who was once Lieutenant-Governor of Iowa. He got that job because he could scrub stairs until they were squeaky-clean. And while he worked for the Scotts, Billy went to high school where he became well-known as a runner. Some time later he took up baseball, and right from his first game it was clear he was a winner.

'Are you Billy Sunday?' he was asked, after a baseball game.

'That's me,' he said. 'But who are you?'

'My name's Anson, and I'm told you have a future in baseball,'

Billy grinned. 'I can sure play the game,' he agreed.

Anson shook Billy by the hand. 'I'm told you're better than that. In fact, I'm here to persuade you to come to Chicago to join the White Stockings.'

Young Billy Sunday could hardly believe his ears. The White Stockings! They were in the National League! It didn't take him long to make up his mind that he should move to Chicago.

Quite soon after he moved, Billy and his baseball friends came across an open-air preacher when they were out walking one day. They sat down on the grass to listen to what he was saying. Billy was so interested that he went time and time again to hear the preacher. What he heard about God there was no different from what he had learned from his mother, but somehow it suddenly made sense to him. Billy asked the Lord Jesus to be his Saviour, and promised to serve him all of his life.

'I guess the guys in the team will laugh at me now,' he thought. 'But I'm not going to hide that I'm a Christian.'

Instead of laughing at him, Billy discovered that his team-mates treated him with real respect.

The White Stockings certainly respected Billy's baseball.

'Tell me about your famous save,' a friend asked, having missed a memorable afternoon.

Billy grinned. 'OK,' he said, 'this is how it happened. I saw Charley swing hard, and heard the bat crack as he met the ball square on the nose. As I saw it rise in the air

I knew it was going clear over my head into the crowd that overflowed on to the field. I could judge within ten feet of where the ball would land, so I turned my back on it and ran, and as I ran, I yelled, "Get out of the way!" The crowd opened like the Red Sea for the rod of Moses. And as I flew over the dirt I prayed to God to help me. Jumping the bench I stopped where I thought the ball would fall. Looking back I saw it going over my head. I jumped and shoved my left hand out. The ball hit it and stuck! I was going so fast I fell under some horses, but I hung on to the ball. You should have heard the crowd yell!'

Billy's friend laughed aloud. 'I can just see it!' he said. 'What a catch!'

'Billy Sunday's speaking at the Young Men's Christian Association,' one boy told another. 'Would you like to come?'

His friend looked surprised. 'You mean the Billy Sunday, the baseball player?'

'The very one! Are you coming?'

'Try to stop me!'

Right from when he became a Christian, Billy wanted to tell other people about the Lord. He was as enthusiastic when he was talking about Jesus as he was when playing the game. And before long, he was well-known for his preaching too.

In the spring of 1888, Billy was sold by the Chicago White Stockings to the Pittsburg team. This was a great move for baseball, but it meant that he and his girlfriend would be separated, but not for long. They were married that September, and lived in Pittsburgh for two-and-a-half years until Billy decided to give up baseball and become a full-time preacher.

'Funny,' Billy said to his wife one day, 'I thought preachers only preached. It didn't occur to me that I'd spend my time putting up tents, organising great choirs of singers, and touring shops, offices and factories!'

His wife smiled. 'That's because you're not a regular preacher,' she said. 'Regular preachers stand in the same pulpit every week, you go all over the place and take your tent with you!'

'Jesus told the paralysed man to take up his bed and walk,' Billy commented. 'It seems he's telling me to take up my tent and preach.'

Along with another well-known preacher, Billy toured several states of America.

'Tell me about your father,' Helen asked her dad one day, several years later.

Helen was Billy's only daughter. She had two brothers, George and little Billy Junior, and then there was a baby on the way.

'I never knew my papa,' Billy explained. 'He died just months before I was born.'

'It must have been sad not to have a dad,' said Helen.

'I didn't know any different,' her father explained. 'And my grandfather was very good to me.'

'Is it because you didn't have a dad yourself that you try to do so much with us?'

Billy gave a sigh of relief and hugged his dark-haired daughter. What she said pleased him a lot, because he was away from home so often he sometimes felt as though he was neglecting his children. But Helen at least didn't seem to think that was the case.

'Want a game of ball?' he asked.

Helen and George were up like a shot!

'Were there really ten thousand at the meeting?' George asked his father, when he heard the news.

'There really were,' laughed Billy. 'And there were some outside that couldn't get in.'

'Did you really have electric light?' the boy queried.

'Yes we did! The place was bright as a summer's day, so bright the light almost dazzled me when I was preaching!'

'I'd love to see electric light,' George said wistfully.

'You would?' said Billy. 'Then get your sister and brother and I'll show you what it looks like.'

Billy took the children with him to the building in which he'd been preaching and asked the caretaker to switch on the lights.

'How did that happen?' George gasped. 'Nobody did anything!'

Billy explained that electric lights worked from a switch, and he even allowed the children to switch them on and off.

'You're a great dad,' Helen said, squeezing her father's hand.

Billy thought back to his own childhood and to his four long years in the orphan school, and returned Helen's hand squeeze with lots of love. As they walked back home, George asked his father where his next preaching meetings were to be. Billy told him, and said he was going there by train.

'I love travelling by train,' George said.

Billy thought back over the years to his first train journey, and told his children about when he was sent away to school and didn't see his mother for four whole years.

'That must have been an awful train journey,' Helen sympathised.

'It was,' agreed Billy, 'but I made up for it long ago with many happy train journeys. I guess that was the start of my travelling.'

Billy Sunday spent his life going from place to place holding Christian campaigns. The meetings he spoke at grew until the average attendance was more than 20,000. Over the years he spoke to several million people. But not all of them went to hear the good news about Jesus. At one meeting in Springfield, Illinois, a man jumped out of the crowd brandishing a great whip that he used to lash Billy Sunday across the knees. But the poor man had forgotten how athletic the preacher was, and he must have got the biggest surprise of his life when Billy leapt off the platform and on to him before he could lash out at anyone else. For the next few weeks, Billy had to preach at his meetings holding himself up with crutches, not because of the damage the whip did, but because he sprained his ankle when he'd landed on the attacker!

'Did you hear what Billy Sunday said?' John asked his friend one day.

'What was that?' Tom asked.

'He says that if you live wrong you can't die right.'

'Well that's true enough,' Tom said. 'He has a real way with words.'

Puzzled by the expression on his friend's face, John asked if Tom had ever heard Billy Sunday preach.

'I sure have,' his friend replied. 'And if I hadn't you wouldn't see me here today.'

'Why's that?'

'I'll tell you why,' Tom said, sitting down on a wall at the roadside. 'You know me as a respectable businessman, and so I am. But when I went to hear Billy Sunday I was a broken-down drunk. And if there is something that man can't abide it's drink.'

'I know,' John said. 'I've heard him speak on the subject.'

'So have I,' Tom told his friend. 'And my life has never been the same since. That night I asked the Lord Jesus to wash away all my sins, and he did just that. Over the months that followed Jesus helped me give up drink, and build up my business again. I thank God for Billy Sunday, and I thank the Lord Jesus for what he's done for me every day of my life!'

In 1935, when America's baseball preacher died, there were men and women, boys and girls, right across the country who thanked God for Billy Sunday, and who thanked God for the message of Christ's love and salvation that he had brought to them.

Fact File: *Baseball.*
Billy Sunday played baseball for the Chicago White Stockings, one of the most famous baseball teams in America. (Today they are usually called the Chicago White Sox.)

Baseball has been played in America since 1839, and the first organised club was founded in 1845. Today it is played by a large number of professional clubs across America, and by lots of amateurs in America and beyond. Although Billy was paid to play for the White Stockings, players today receive much more money than they did in the past. Baseball is a big business in America.

 Keynote: Billy was afraid that his team-mates would make fun of him because he had become a Christian, but he decided to tell them anyway. He found that they actually respected him rather than laughing at him.

It is not always easy to let people know that we believe in Jesus

Christ, but Jesus has suffered so much for us. He even died on the cross for us. We do not have any right to be ashamed of him.

 Think: Billy had heard the gospel message from his mother many times before, but it made sense to him in a new and exciting way when he listened to the open-air preacher. This shows that we should keep listening to explanations of what God has done even when we haven't understood the message in the past. Think about the parts of the Bible that you find hard to understand. Who could explain them to you again?

 Prayer: Lord Jesus, thank you for using all sorts of people in your kingdom. Help me to remember how great you are, and not to be embarrassed to tell my friends that I believe in you. Thank you for all the different people who preach your gospel. Please help me to listen to you carefully. Amen.

Charles H. Spurgeon

Charles was positively jumping with excitement.

'We're nearly there!' he said. 'It's just two more miles to Stambourne!'

His father smiled.

'Does it feel as though you are coming back home when you come here?' the man asked.

Ten-year-old Charles thought about that.

'I suppose it does, in a way,' he said. 'After all, I did stay here with Grandad and Grandma until I was five, and I've been back for every summer holiday since then.'

'True enough,' commented Mr Spurgeon. 'But what do you like best about it?'

The boy laughed.

'I love Grandad and Grandma, and I love the house too,' he explained. 'It's so big and rambling that I can always find hideaway places. My favourite part in the house is a secret.'

'Even to me?' asked his father.

'I suppose not,' Charles laughed. 'It's a little dark room off one of the bedrooms. There are shelves of books all the way around it and piles of them on the floor. Going in there is like entering a treasure chest.'

'Have you found any treasures there?' queried Mr Spurgeon.

'Yes,' the lad said, excitedly. 'There's a book full of stories about people who were killed because they were Christians. But my favourite book of them all is 'The Pilgrim's Progress'. Christian, he's the main character in the story, had all kinds of adventures. In one of them he has to walk between roaring lions to get where God wants him to go. He's scared stiff, but then a man who lives nearby shouts to him and tells him to stay right in the middle of the path and he'll be safe because the lions are chained and they can't reach the middle of the path. So he does that, and walks right between the lions! You should see the drawings in the book, Dad,' he added, 'the lions are really ferocious!'

Mr Spurgeon smiled at his son.

'I know,' he said. 'I read that book when I was about your age, and I remember the lions well.'

Charles's grandfather was a minister, and during that summer holiday he had a representative of the London Missionary Society staying with him for a short visit while he was taking some meetings near Stambourne. His name was Richard Knill.

'Mr Knill's very interesting,' Charles told his grandfather. 'I like listening to the stories he tells.'

'He is indeed' old Mr Spurgeon agreed. 'And I think he enjoys your company too.'

'How do you know that?' the boy enquired.

His grandfather smiled. 'I know because he was asking which room was yours. I think you'll be getting an early morning call tomorrow, and an invitation to go for a walk with your missionary friend.'

The following morning Mr Knill did knock at Charles's door, and they did go for a walk in the garden before breakfast. As they walked, Mr Knill spoke to the lad about God's love. Before they returned to the house, the missionary prayed with Charles, asking God that the boy would soon know the Lord, and that he would grow up to be God's faithful servant.

'This child will one day preach the gospel,' Mr Knill told Charles's grandfather, 'and he will preach it to multitudes of people.'

In 1848, when Charles was 14 years old, he was sent to a Church of England school at Maidstone.

'What's your name?' one of his teachers asked, soon after he arrived.

'Spurgeon, sir,' the boy replied.

'No, no,' the teacher responded. 'What's your name?'

'Charles Spurgeon, sir.'

Shaking his head, the teacher said, 'I just need your Christian name lad.'

'Please, sir,' was the reply. 'I'm afraid I don't have one.'

'Why is that?' asked the man.

Charles answered what he knew to be true. 'It's because I don't think I'm a Christian.'

While he was not a Christian when he went to school at 14, he became one the following year.

One Sunday, Charles was on his way to church when a terrible snowstorm forced him to shelter in a little church he had never been in before, and it wasn't one that appealed to him.

'The minister didn't arrive,' he told someone later, 'I suppose he was snowed up. One of the men in the church took his place, and at first I thought he was very stupid. He had to stick to the text he'd taken from the Bible because he seemed to have nothing else to say. His text was "Look to me, and be saved, all the ends of the earth." He kept repeating, "Look! Look! Look!"'

'That must have been pretty boring,' Charles's friend commented.

'It was at first,' the boy replied, 'but then he really made me look to Christ. He made me think about Christ on the cross, then dead and buried and raised from the dead, and now alive forever in heaven. After about ten minutes he stopped because he'd run out of things to say.'

His friend smiled. 'That must have been a relief.'

Charles ignored the comment and continued. 'When he'd finished the man looked right at me and spoke right to me.'

'Embarrassing or what!' his friend laughed.

Again Charles ignored him.

'Young man,' he said, right to me, 'look to Jesus Christ. Look! Look! You have nothing to do but to look and live!'

'And?' asked his friend.

'It suddenly all made sense. It was as though a wonderful light had been switched on. I became a Christian that day, and I now know for sure that Jesus is my Saviour.'

Charles' friend looked at him. 'Are you being serious?' he asked.

'Never more so,' said Charles. 'I've never been more serious and I've never been happier.'

Just two years later, in 1851, seventeen-year-old Charles became pastor of a small church, and two years later he moved to New Park Street Chapel in London. Before long he was the talk of the town, and the church became far too small for all the people who came to hear him preach.

'This is a terrible time to be a minister in London,' thought Charles, in 1854, as he walked home after a funeral. 'Now that cholera is sweeping through the city again it just seems to be one funeral after another. And the disease hits people so hard and so suddenly that most die within hours of becoming ill. While I know that the Christians in my congregation go home to the Lord when they die, my heart breaks at the thought of those who die without hope.'

A horse trotted along the road, and as it passed the young minister saw that it was trailing a cart full of rough coffins, no doubt full of more victims of cholera. He turned away from them and found himself looking into the window of a shoemaker's shop. There was a card in the window, and he read it aloud.

'If you make the Most High your dwelling – even the Lord, who is my refuge – then no harm will befall you, no disaster will come near your tent.'

As he read the verse, which comes from Psalm 91, a great peace flowed through Charles's heart and mind. He knew he could go on, and he knew that having with God with him he should not fear any evil. In fact, God gave him a very precious gift to encourage him, as he married Susannah*, a young woman in his congregation. Their life together was a most beautiful love story.

Thomas Medhurst, who was converted through Charles's preaching, started preaching himself as soon as he became a Christian. That was around 1854. Spurgeon worked with him for part of each week, training the younger man as well as being helped by him. Soon other young men came for training. By 1861, he had 20 students, two years later there were 66, and some of the following years topped over 100! That was the beginning of The Pastors' College.

'Tell me about your students,' a visitor asked Charles, in the mid 1870s. 'Are they all from London?'

Spurgeon smiled at the thought.

'One man walked from the highlands of Scotland to study here, but the rest come from all over England, and beyond.'

'That's all very well for those who can spare the time to study,' the visitor commented. 'Not everyone is free to do that.'

---

* Susannah Spurgeon's story is included in Ten Girls who made a difference.

'True enough,' Spurgeon agreed. 'That's why we run evening classes too. Between one and two hundred people attend them.'

As the college was growing, so the congregation was growing too. In fact, New Park Street Chapel was bursting at the seams. In 1856, which was the year The Pastors' College began, work started on the building of a huge new church, the Metropolitan Tabernacle. It was opened in 1861.

'I'm told that there were 6,000 people in church today,' Susannah commented to her husband, one Sunday evening. 'I'm sure that's right because the place was absolutely full.'

Charles was relaxing on one side of the fire with four-year-old Thomas nearly sleeping on his knee. And Susannah was on the other side, with Thomas's twin brother, Charles.

'And,' went on Susannah, 'I hear that your sermons are being printed in more than twenty languages, including Russian, Chinese, Japanese and Arabic.'

'That's all true,' her husband said. 'And I'm really grateful for that. But I hope and pray that people are more anxious to hear what God has to say than what I have to say.'

'Yes indeed,' agreed Susannah. 'But I still think it is good to remember the ways in which God is using you.'

'Only so long as it doesn't make me proud,' added her husband seriously.

Susannah grinned. 'I'll soon tell you if it does!'

Charles took the sleepy Thomas and put him to bed, and his twin was soon sound asleep beside him. Tired out after preaching, Spurgeon suggested an early night for them too. Before they went to bed, the pair of them continued to think through the things they had to thank God for.

'We should thank God that as well as the 6,000 who hear you preach, your sermons are being sent all round the world,' said Susannah. 'They are also being printed every week in some American newspapers! Did you hear how many of your leaflets were given out to university students?'

Spurgeon shook his head.

'I understand that it was over 150,000.'

Kneeling by his chair, Charles commented to his wife. 'I wanted an early night, but you've reminded me of so many things to thank God for that we might be on our knees praying for quite some time!'

'It's all very well for famous preachers to stand up in church and talk week after week after week. All they do is talk, they don't actually get down to the business of helping people in need,' said John Smith, who had been invited to go to a service in the Metropolitan Tabernacle. 'You show me a man that does good works and I'll come and hear him preach.'

The old man who had invited the stranger in smiled. 'Then let's go for a walk together. I'll tell you some of the things Mr Spurgeon has done, and I'm quite sure you'll want to come to the service this evening.'

It was 1873, and Charles had been the old man's minister for twenty years. As the two men walked, the story that unfolded kept John Smith interested for the whole afternoon.

'Charles Spurgeon has always been generous to the poor, often leaving himself poor as a result. He encouraged the congregation to help too, and said that the Metropolitan Tabernacle should take up some work with children. In the church magazine, The Sword and Trowel, he suggested the opening of a Christian school. A lady called Mrs Hillyard saw the article and wrote saying that she thought the church should open an orphanage, and that she would give £20,000 towards it.'

'That's a lot of money,' commented John Smith.

'So it is,' the old man said. 'When Mr Spurgeon went to visit Mrs Hillyard and saw that she lived in a very ordinary house, he thought she'd made a mistake in the letter. "We've called about the £200 you mentioned in your letter," Spurgeon said. "Did I write £200?" Mrs Hillyard replied. "I meant £20,000." The minister questioned the lady carefully to see if her money should be left to some family members, but there were none. So the £20,000 was accepted and used to open the Stockwell Orphanage for Boys.'

'You were right,' John Smith said. 'Your minister does seem to live like a Christian as well as talk like one. I will come along to the evening service with you.'

That was John Smith's first visit to the Metropolitan Tabernacle, but it was not his last. He was still attending in 1880, when the Stockwell Orphanage for Girls was opened. There were many people in London like John Smith, men and women who were brought by friends to hear Charles Spurgeon, and others who came just out of interest. Often they came with no faith, and many left having found Jesus Christ as their Saviour. Among them were some of the hundreds of children who lived in the Stockwell Orphanages.

Fact File: *Cholera.* Spurgeon was a minister in London during several cholera epidemics in the mid-19th century. Cholera is an infectious disease that can spread very easily through contaminated water supplies. Getting clean water was a real problem in cities at that time because they had grown so quickly. Once the connection between dirty water and cholera was discovered, laws were passed to encourage new water supplies and reservoirs to be developed.

Keynote: Spurgeon was a very famous man. You might even call him a superstar preacher. Many people came to hear him preach, and many more read his sermons. But he realised that these were things that should make him thank God rather than be proud of his own ability. We need to remember to thank God for all our successes, and to remember that they come from him rather than ourselves.

Think: John Smith was impressed with Spurgeon because he was living out the things that he told other people to do. Spurgeon was willing to make himself poor so that he could help other people. It is important that we believe the things that we read in the Bible, but it is also important that we obey it. Think of ways in which you can put the Bible teaching you have received into practice.

Prayer: Lord Jesus, thank you for all the skills and talents that you have given me. Thank you for the chances that I have to help others. Please help me to know you as my Saviour just as Spurgeon did, and teach me to give praise and thanks to you for all the good things that are in my life. Amen.

Aiden W. Tozer

'I don't believe it!' Mr Tozer said, as the lamb was born. 'This little thing has got three ears!'

His son came running at this interesting news, and watched as the newborn lamb nuzzled its mother. But the sheep edged away from it, and pushed the tiny creature aside.

'I must have given her a fright when I shouted for you,' the farmer told Aiden. 'Let's give the pair of them some peace to get to know each other. You check on her in half-an-hour.'

Aiden went back to give his pig a new bed of straw. Her ears twitched when the boy spoke to her. 'I remember when you were young,' he told the sow. 'You were half-starved and looked fit for nothing. You'd never know that now,' he added, clapping the sow's sturdy shoulder, 'you've grown into a fine old girl.'

Having replaced the pig's bedding and filled her water trough, Aiden went back to see how the new lamb was getting on.

'She'll be licked dry by now and full of her mother's first milk,' he thought, as he crossed the field.

But she was not. The lamb was standing alone, wet and miserable, and the sheep was a good distance off and looking cross. Aiden picked the little thing up and took her to the sheep. The lamb tried to nuzzle her mother, but every time they got close, the ewe nudged her baby away. Aiden took off his jacket, picked up the lamb and wrapped it round her.

'She doesn't seem to want you,' he told the tiny creature, 'I wonder if she doesn't recognise a lamb with three ears.'

'What have you got there?' Mrs Tozer asked, when the boy took his bundle into the kitchen.

'It's a lamb with three ears,' he explained, 'and her mother won't accept her.'

'Bring the poor creature here,' said the woman, 'and let me have a look at her.'

Aiden handed the lamb over.

'She's shivering with cold and fright,' the boy commented. 'Will I heat some milk for her?'

'There's no need to do that,' explained Mrs Tozer, 'your brother is milking the cows and the milk will still be warm. Go and get some for her.'

Taking a jug from the shelf, Aiden went to the cowshed and collected some milk. He put it into a bottle they kept for orphan lambs and very soon the bottle was empty and the lamb was full. She stopped shivering too.

'May I look after this one?' the boy asked.

'She's all yours,' laughed Mrs Tozer, 'and she'll make a good sheep, I'm sure. Look how you rescued that scraggy pig and built her up to be a good 'un.'

'Aiden's got a kind heart,' Mr Tozer told his wife that night, after the children had gone to bed. 'But he can pick a fight in an empty field. I reckon he's the most argumentative boy in La Jose, Pennsylvania!'

'He's just like my mother,' said Mrs Tozer. 'And that's not a compliment.'

Just then Aiden came into the room. He had woken up and wanted to check how the lamb was.

'Did you hear what we were saying?' his father asked.

The boy had, but wondered whether to admit it or not.

'You did, didn't you?'

He bowed his head.

'I just don't understand you, son,' his father said wearily. 'You're as gentle as can be with helpless creatures, and as argumentative as a bear with a sore head with other people.'

Aiden opened his mouth to argue with his father, but decided that would not be a good idea.

Not long afterwards, Aiden and his sister Essie were swinging high up in their apple tree. The gloriously sunny day had brought the boy out in a very good mood, so good that he started to sing a Sunday school song.

'Is there any room in heaven for a little lad like me?' he sang aloud, 'Is there any room in heaven for me?'

From the other side of the bushes under the tree, his neighbour's voice yelled back, 'If there's going to be any room for you in heaven you'll have to mend your ways.'

Essie started to giggle, but stopped as soon as she saw the thunderous look in her brother's eyes.

'I dreamed our house burned down,' Aiden told his parents one morning at breakfast time. 'I wonder what the dream meant.'

'You're getting as bad as your grandma,' Mr Tozer said. 'She's forever telling us the meaning of her dreams.'

But that dream made a deep impression on young Aiden, so much so that he worked out how he could save his brother and sisters if the house were to go on fire. Just a few months later, that's exactly what happened. Ten-year-old Aiden carried out the plan he had made and led his younger brother and his sisters to the safety of the woods.

Even his next-door neighbour admitted that the boy was a hero that day in 1907!

'I've made a decision,' Aiden announced some time later. 'I hate my name and I don't want to be called Aiden ever again.'

'But it's a good name,' his mother protested. 'You were called after the storekeeper, and his wife's a good friend of mine.'

'I don't care!' the boy said crossly. 'From now on I'll not answer to Aiden ever again! I'll just answer to AW. My initials are much better than my name.'

And from then on, that's what he did. Aiden Wilson Tozer was AW for the rest of his life.

One day, when AW was not quite 18, he was in town and came upon a crowd at a busy street corner.

'I wonder what's going on here,' he said to himself, as he pushed his way through the crowd, till he stood in front of an elderly man who was speaking about Jesus.

'If you don't know how to be saved,' the preacher shouted, 'just call on God, saying "Lord be merciful to me a sinner."'

The words spun round in AW's mind. As he walked home all sorts of things went through his head. He remembered the arguments and fights he'd been in. And at the same time he remembered what his father's mother had told him about the Lord.'

'Am I really a sinner?' AW asked himself. 'Do I really need to be saved? Am I that bad?'

When he arrived home, he went into the attic to sort himself out. And by the time he climbed down the stairs he was a changed young man. He had asked God for forgiveness, and had become a Christian. That very day his parents noticed a difference in him, and before long he was the talk of the town.

'I don't know what's happened to AW,' a neighbour told her husband, 'but he's as kind to people now as he's always been to animals, and that's saying something!'

In 1919, AW became pastor of the Alliance Church in Nutter Fort, West Virginia and went there to live with his young wife, Ada. In the ten years that followed he was a minister in Ohio, Indiana and Chicago. By the time they moved to Chicago, where they were to remain for over thirty years, there were seven young Tozers, six boys and a baby girl.

'The elders offered me an increase in my salary,' AW told his wife, after a meeting at the church. The children were young at the time, and Mrs Tozer had to work very hard to make ends meet.

'You didn't accept it, did you?' she asked.

AW smiled. 'No,' he assured her. 'I didn't, though you would have had no trouble spending it I'm sure. But when we were married we promised each other and the Lord that we'd rely on him for all our needs, and he's never let us down.'

Thinking of the children's shoes that were becoming too small, Mrs Tozer nodded agreement. 'The Lord will supply all our needs,' she said firmly. 'And I look forward to seeing how he does it.'

Just then she noticed that the knees of AW's trousers were wearing thin. Mrs Tozer smiled. 'Some people wear through the seats of their trousers by lounging around,' she thought. 'But my husband wears through the knees by spending so much time in prayer.'

AW went through to his study and knelt by his chair. He also knew the children needed shoes, and he prayed that God would provide them.

'Thank you, Father, for giving all we need,' he finished, knowing for a certainty that God would hear and answer his prayer.

'Dad,' his eldest son said, as they walked to the railway station to meet a friend off the train, 'why don't we get a car? You travel miles and miles to preach at meetings.'

'We don't have a car because we don't need one,' AW said.

His son thought about that. 'Can we only have things we need?' he asked. 'Can we not sometimes have things just because we want them?'

AW strode along beside the boy. 'I hope we do give you treats,' he said, 'but I don't feel the need for them myself. All I need is my family about me, enough food to eat, warm clothes to wear, and my books.'

His son thought about that as they neared the station. 'It's quite true,' he decided. 'Dad does only buy what is absolutely necessary for himself, though we do get treats from time to time.'

Although the boy didn't know it, his parents had so little money that they didn't even have a bank account.

'What's Dad doing?' Rebecca asked her mother, when she came home from school one day.

'I'll give you three guesses,' one of her brothers teased. 'In fact,' he went on, 'I'll give you three things to choose from. Is he writing a book, or is he writing a book, or is he writing a book?'

Rebecca pretended to think about the answer, and then she grinned. 'I think... I think he's writing a book.'

'First prize to Rebecca Tozer,' her brother laughed. 'She got the right answer first time!'

'How many has he written now?' she asked.

The boy shook his head. 'I've no idea, but it must be more than a dozen.'

'His older brother looked up from his homework. 'Much more,' he said, then looked down again.

For once the young Tozers were wrong, their father was not writing a book, he was writing a letter. It was in reply to one he had received from a boy he had met at a youth camp. AW was a favourite of the young people at Christian camps.

'I greatly enjoyed meeting you at Canby Camp,' he wrote, 'and hope to hear good things about you as the years go on. Learn to discipline yourself like a prize fighter or big league ball player. Most boys are too soft and don't like to do anything they don't enjoy doing. Sometimes we have to do what we don't like and that is good for us. Abraham Lincoln was a good example of a man who started young to learn everything he could. If he had wasted his time loafing he would not have become the great man he was.'

AW signed the letter and folded it into its envelope.

'It's strange,' he thought, 'a letter to a boy I met a camp might be every bit as important as the book I'm going to work on now, if it helps show him how to live for the Lord.'

It was a summer evening, and he worked until the sun had nearly set before going through to be with his family.

'Does everyone's father work as hard as you do?' his youngest son, Stanley, asked.

Mrs Tozer wondered what the answer to that question would be.

'I don't suppose they do,' AW told the boy. 'But not everyone has the best news in the world to pass on, and it seems a shame to waste any time by not doing it. If you had good news you'd want to pass it on right away, wouldn't you?'

'If my team won a ball game, I would tell everyone I met,' Stanley agreed. 'So that's why you spend so much time in your study preparing sermons and writing books, and why you go to camps as well.'

'That's right,' said his father.

'But will you never take a holiday, ever?' the boy asked. All his friends' fathers took holidays with their families.

'I've never had a holiday. I don't feel the need. A preaching tour or young people's camp is better for me than a holiday.'

Stanley thought about that, and decided that if he had children he would take them on holidays that weren't all about work.

AW had already prepared his Sunday sermons one week in May 1963, when he suffered a heart attack. The sermons were never preached, because he died late that evening. When the news broke, Christians in many countries of the world remembered the man who had taught them how to live for Christ. And many others looked at the row of books on their bookshelves written by AW Tozer. Some people had two shelves of his books, for he wrote over forty. That was quite amazing, because AW never went to college; he just studied God's Word, the Bible.

Fact File: *Publishing.*

AW was very well known because of the large numbers of books that he wrote. Many ministers and preachers have been able to reach thousands of people through books. These are people whom they could never have spoken to in person.

In fact, some people regard the development of the printing press as one of the major factors that helped the Reformation in the 16th century. The printing press allowed lots of books to be produced at once for the first time. Until then, every copy had to be written out by hand.

 Keynote: AW never felt the need of a holiday because he was so enthusiastic about spreading 'the best news in the world'. When people have good news, they want to share it with others, especially with their friends.

The whole purpose of AW's efforts in preaching, camps and books was to tell people the good news about Jesus. In doing that, he was fulfilling one of the main jobs that Jesus left with his disciples just before he ascended to heaven.

 Think: AW wrote to the boy from the camp about the need for discipline. Sometimes we need to do things that we don't want to do at the time. We do them knowing that they will be good for us in the future.

AW used training to be a baseball player as an example, in the Bible Paul used the example of a runner in a race. Think about ways in which you can discipline yourself and try hard for God.

 Prayer: Lord Jesus, thank you for being willing to leave the glory of heaven to live and die so that people can be saved from their sins. Thank you for those who tell us about you, and for the effort that they put into doing this. Please help me to try hard to discipline myself in serving you. Amen.

Martyn Lloyd-Jones

Martyn Lloyd-Jones looked out the window of the train.

'Are we nearly there?' he asked.

His father smiled. 'We've a long way to go yet. But we're just coming up to a very important stage in the journey.'

The boy looked out the window. 'We're not in anywhere,' he said.

'We are,' Mr Lloyd-Jones told his son. 'We're in Wales, and before very long we'll cross the border into England.'

Martyn sat with his nose nearly touching the train window. A few miles further on his father told him that they were crossing the border.

'But it looks just the same,' the lad said, sounding a little disappointed. 'It's just hills and trees and fields like we have at home.'

Mr Lloyd-Jones smiled at his son. 'Not quite the same,' he said, in his lovely Welsh accent. 'There's nowhere in the world quite like Wales.'

Martyn didn't want to argue with his father, but to his eight-year-old eyes England looked much the same as home.

'Wake up,' Mr Lloyd-Jones said, giving his son a shake. 'We're nearly in London.'

Martyn jumped, then looked out the window as the train snaked through the suburbs and into the centre of the city.

'There are a lot of houses here,' he said. 'There must be thousands of people in London.'

'Millions,' corrected his father. 'And there's the river,' he added, pointing to the left.

'That's the Thames!' Martyn said excitedly. 'In geography we learned that the first people to live here came to trade on the River Thames.'

'You're a clever boy,' his father told him, then laughed. 'Maybe one day you'll come to London. A lot of Welsh boys come here to work.'

Martyn shook his head. 'I don't think I will. There are too many people here already.'

When they climbed out of the train and tried to walk along the crowded platform, Martyn thought back to what he had said. 'There are too many people here already,' just seemed to describe the station platform perfectly. It was exciting, but he was glad that he would be catching a train back home on Saturday, after they had been to the agricultural show.

On Friday something happened to change their plans. One of the most important men in their home village of Llangeitho, in Cardiganshire, sent them a message to say he was in London to buy a car and he would give them a run home!

'Wait till I tell my brothers!' thought Martyn.

His father laughed. 'Imagine the pair of us arriving back in Llangeitho in the squire's car! It'll be like royalty coming to town.'

But it didn't turn out to be quite like that. Although the car was a grand one, it was not in good condition. Their first puncture happened before they left London, the next one not long afterwards, and there were others after that. When they eventually drew near their home village, Martyn whispered to his father.

'How many miles is it from London to here?'

'About 300,' his father whispered back.

'And how long has it taken us to come by car?'

His father winked at him. 'It's taken from 5.30 pm on Saturday till 9 pm on Monday. You can work out how long that is for yourself.'

'That's you home safe and sound, if rather later than expected,' announced the squire, from the front seat of the car.

Martyn's brothers couldn't wait to hear about London, and about the car journey home. He told of his travels and adventures, punctures and all.

'I'm not going back to London,' he finished. 'There are too many people there already, and it's too far away from Llangeitho.'

Six years later, in 1914, Martyn was back in London, though he longed to be home in Wales. His family had moved for business reasons. From a small town where everyone knew everyone else, and all that was going on, the three Lloyd-Jones boys found themselves strangers in a vast city at war. However, there was a little of Wales in London, at Charing Cross Chapel, and that's where the family went to church.

'What subjects interest you?' one of his new school teachers asked Martyn.

'I like history and English, Sir,' the teenager replied. 'But my best subject is science, and I want to study medicine.'

The teacher nodded his head. 'You'll have to work hard if you hope to be a doctor.'

Martyn did work hard, both at school and in his father's dairy business. At the age of 16 he became a medical student at St Bartholomew's Hospital in London, one of the most famous teaching hospitals in the world. It was while he was a medical student there, that Martyn began to think seriously about what he believed.

'I don't know exactly when I became a Christian,' he told a friend at church. 'Over a period of time it just became clear to me that what the Bible says is true; that I needed a Saviour and that he is Jesus Christ.'

'Can you not remember a day when you decided to become a Christian?' asked his friend.

Martyn shook his head. 'No,' he said. 'I cannot. Some people, like the Apostle Paul, have sudden and dramatic conversions. I did not, and that doesn't make me any less of a Christian.'

In January 1927, Dr Martyn Lloyd-Jones married Dr Bethan Phillips.* They met in church. Bethan was also of Welsh descent.

'What does your wife think of you giving up medicine?' a colleague asked Martyn, on hearing that his friend had made that decision.

Lloyd-Jones shook his head. 'I'm not giving up medicine,' he corrected, 'I'm taking up preaching. Bethan and I have discussed this and prayed about it, and she is as clear

---

* The story of Bethan Lloyd Jones is included in Ten Girls who made a differnce.

in her mind as I am that we are doing the right thing.'

'But you're a very clever doctor,' objected his colleague. 'It seems such a waste.'

Martyn took a long breath before answering.

'My patients have medical problems, and I can often help them. But they also have a spiritual problem that no medicine can help. They have the problem of sin, and sin is a terminal disease. They will die of it. But if they accept the Lord Jesus as their Saviour, they will rise again and spend forever in heaven with him. Is that not better medicine than aspirin?'

His colleague had nothing more to say.

Soon after their wedding Martyn and Bethan Lloyd-Jones set off for their new home in the Welsh town of Aberavon, where Martyn became minister of Sandfields Church.

'Dear Mother,' Martyn wrote, after they had been in Sandfields for a year, 'God has been so good to us since we came here. The church is growing, and not only with respectable people who want to come and hear the gospel. Some well-known drunkards were converted, and the difference in their lives was so marked that they were the talk of the town. Of course, that brought more people in, and some of them have since become Christians. Ordinary working men and women are finding their way to Sandfields, and many of them are really searching for the truth. Bethan runs a Bible class for women, and I have one for men.'

Not only did Martyn's reputation as a teacher spread through Aberavon, people all over Wales heard about the young doctor turned minister.

Having moved to London as a boy the year the First World War broke out, Martyn, Bethan and their two young daughters moved back there just months before the outbreak of the Second World War. He was to become one of the two ministers in Westminster Chapel. Although the war was raging all around them, the congregation continued to meet for worship every week.

'I can hear a flying bomb,' a lady thought, during one Sunday morning service.

The noise of the bomb grew louder and louder, then there was the dreaded silence.

'It's very near,' she worried, as she waited to hear from which direction the explosion came.

There was a minute of silence between flying bombs cutting out and landing.

Suddenly there was a terrific explosion. The flying bomb had landed not far from the church. Everyone in the building closed their eyes, many in prayer and some in terrible fear. The building shuddered, and a fine white dust fell from its walls and ceiling and covered the whole congregation.

Opening her eyes, the woman looked round in shocked amazement at the white covered people around her.

'I'm in heaven!' she thought. 'I've died and gone to heaven!'

But as the people in the congregation began to rub the dust out of their eyes, she realised that she was still very much on earth!

Every Friday night, the Doctor (as Martyn was most often called) held discussion classes in Westminster Chapel. Eventually too many people were attending for discussions to take place, and he started preaching instead. Some of the sermons the Doctor preached on Friday evenings are now published in books that are read in many countries of the world.

Martyn Lloyd-Jones also became involved in Inter-Varsity Fellowship, an organisation for university students. He was often asked to speak at students' meetings.

'I believe in the theory of evolution,' a student told Martyn before a meeting.

'Then you are a brave man,' the Doctor replied. 'I would not like to base my life on a theory which is not based on truth, when I could base it on the Word of God who never tells lies.'

The student looked shocked.

'You're a doctor,' he said, 'and you've studied science. How can you then ignore what scientists tell us about how the world was made?'

'Young man,' said Martyn, 'if I want to know about something, should I ask the person who made it or someone else who had only used it?'

'The maker, I suppose,' agreed the student. 'But you can't ask God questions about how he made the universe.'

'I don't need to,' the Doctor replied. 'God has told us how he made it. Go home and read the first few chapters of the Bible and you'll find out for yourself.'

An hour later, as Martyn finished his talk to the students, he told them that he had just one more thing he wanted to say.

'It seems that some of you are in danger of making science your god, and that is a very dangerous thing to do. Science is the process of discovering what God has made in his wonderful creation. All science does is find out about God through what he has made. Nothing science discovers will ever prove that God doesn't exist. If it seems to do that, it is not true science, it is a lie.'

The Doctor sat down. And there was one student in the audience who was very quiet. He knew that it was because of him Martyn had said what he did.

'I need to go home and think about this,' the young man said to himself. 'And I'd better read the beginning of the Bible too. I might even go along to Westminster Chapel.'

The following Sunday, the student headed for the City of London. He had thought about what the Doctor said, and wanted to hear him preach.

'What kind of people will go to his church?' he wondered, as he walked along the road. 'I imagine they will all be well-off and clever.'

There was a surprise in store for him, and he told a fellow student about it the next day.

'The place was packed! There were some very wealthy looking people there,' he said. 'But there were one or two faces I knew from the theatre too. I didn't think actors and actresses went to church! And there were a lot of very poor people, some just off the streets.'

In that one visit to Westminster Chapel, the student found out a great deal about the Doctor. Although he was by then a very famous preacher, Martyn Lloyd-Jones cared for everyone, rich or poor, famous or quite unknown. And all kinds of people came to church and became Christians through his preaching.

The Doctor did not just make an impact on those who attended Westminster Chapel and university students. He helped set up an annual conference for ministers, and his encouragement greatly helped a new publishing house, and a Christian library

'Books can go where people cannot,' he told Bethan. 'And the ministers who come to the Westminster Conference and use the Evangelical Library will be here long after I'm in heaven.'

Thirty years after moving to Westminster Chapel, because he became ill, the Doctor felt it was time to retire. But that did not stop him preaching. He was a doctor of souls, and for another thirteen years he continued to preach to people suffering from sin-sickness.

It was in 1981 that the time came for him to die.

'Don't pray for healing,' he told his family. 'Don't try to hold me back from the glory.'

And when he died, he left his family here on earth and went to meet his lovely and loving Lord Jesus in heaven.

Factfile: *The Blitz.*
Martyn was pastor in Westminster Chapel during the Second World War. At that time London was a very dangerous place to be. From mid-1940 until mid-1941, Nazi planes dropped bombs on many cities and towns in Britain, but London was the most heavily bombed. People had to put blankets over their windows at night in case the light would attract the attention of the bombers.

Keynote: Martyn did good work as a doctor. Doctors can help lots of people by using medicine to cure illnesses. But Martyn also knew that the most important disease that we suffer from is sin sickness. No medicine can cure this. What we need is to be forgiven through Jesus' sacrifice for us. Martyn decided that he should tell people about this, even if it meant that he could not work as a doctor anymore.

Think: All sorts of people came to Martyn's church, even people whom we might not expect to go to church at all. The good news about Jesus is for everyone. Martyn mixed with all sorts of people, and he really loved them. The gospel is for everyone. This means you too.

 Prayer: Lord Jesus, thank you for coming to seek and to save all sorts of people. Help me to understand what you have done. Please help me to be kind to all the different people I meet, and to realise that they are all valuable in your sight. Amen.

QUIZ

How much can you remember
about the ten boys who
changed the world?

Try answering these questions
to find out ...

Samuel Rutherford

1. What did Samuel fall down when he was a little boy?
2. Where did Samuel serve God as a minister?
3. What did he want for his congregation?

John Owen

4. How old was John when he started studying at Oxford?
5. Which church did John preach in after the Battle of Dunbar?
6. Which disasters hit London in the 1660s?

Jonathan Edwards

7. What was the town where Jonathan first served as a minister?
8. What happened between 1734 and 1736 and again in 1740?
9. Can you remember the names of any of the Indian tribes that Jonathan became a minister to?

George Whitefield

10. Why did George have a squint in his left eye?
11. Why did George start preaching in the open air?
12. Name three of the places where George went to preach.

Robert Murray McCheyne

13. Where did Robert go to university?
14. What was the name of his brother who died while he was at university?
15. Where did Robert go on a fact-finding trip in 1839?

Dwight L. Moody

16. Which city did Dwight go to so that he could work for his uncle?
17. Which American president visited one of Dwight's schools?
18. What was the name of the singer he teamed up with as he toured around preaching?

Billy Sunday

19. What had happened to Billy's father?
20. Which baseball team did Billy first play for?
21. Which invention intrigued Billy's children?

Charles H. Spurgeon

22. What was Charles' favourite book when he was young?
23. How old was Charles when he first became a minister?
24. What was the name of the big church that was built to replace New Park Street Chapel?

Aiden W. Tozer

25. What was wrong with the lamb whose mother did not want it?
26. Why did the knees on AW's trousers wear out?
27. Why didn't AW have a car?

Martyn Lloyd-Jones

28. Which part of the UK was Martyn from?
29. What did he want to be when he was young?
30. What was the name of the big church in London that he was minister of?

Answers:

1. A well.
2. Anwoth.
3. That they would fall in love with Jesus.
4. 15.
5. St Giles, in Edinburgh.
6. The Great Plague and the Great Fire.
7. Northampton.
8. Lots of people were converted (there was a revival).
9. River Indians/Housatonics, Mohawks and Iroquois.
10. He had a very bad attack of measles when he was a little boy.
11. Many of the churches would not let him preach in their buildings because he was not a member of the Church of England.
12. Any of – England, Scotland, Ireland, Wales, Gibraltar, Bermuda and America.

13. Edinburgh.

14. David.

15. To the Holy Land (Israel).

16. Boston.

17. Abraham Lincoln.

18. Ira Sankey.

19. He died of an illness that he caught in the army before Billy was born.

20. The Chicago White Stockings.

21. The electric light.

22. The Pigrim's Progress.

23. 17.

24. The Metropolitan Tabernacle.

25. It had 3 ears.

26. Because he spent so much time on his knees in prayer.

27. He didn't need one.

28. Wales.

29. A doctor.

30. Westminster Chapel.

Start collecting this series now!

Ten Boys who used their Talents:
ISBN 978-1-84550-146-4

Paul Brand, Ghillean Prance, C.S.Lewis,
C.T. Studd, Wilfred Grenfell, J.S. Bach,
James Clerk Maxwell, Samuel Morse,
George Washington Carver,
John Bunyan.

Ten Girls who used their Talents:
ISBN 978-1-84550-147-1

Helen Roseveare, Maureen McKenna,
Anne Lawson, Harriet Beecher Stowe,
Sarah Edwards, Selina Countess of
Huntingdon, Mildred Cable,
Katie Ann MacKinnon,
Patricia St. John, Mary Verghese.

LIGHT KEEPERS

Ten Boys who Changed the World:
ISBN 978-1-85792-579-1

David Livingstone, Billy Graham,
Brother Andrew,
John Newton, William Carey,
George Müller,
Nicky Cruz, Eric Liddell, Luis Palau,
Adoniram Judson.

Ten Girls who Changed the World:
ISBN 978-1-85792-649-1

Corrie Ten Boom, Mary Slessor,
Joni Eareckson Tada, Isobel Kuhn,
Amy Carmichael, Elizabeth Fry,
Evelyn Brand, Gladys Aylward,
Catherine Booth, Jackie Pullinger.

LIGHT KEEPERS

Ten Boys who Made a Difference:
ISBN 978-1-85792-775-7

Augustine of Hippo, Jan Hus,
Martin Luther, Ulrich Zwingli,
William Tyndale, Hugh Latimer,
John Calvin, John Knox,
Lord Shaftesbury, Thomas Chalmers.

Ten Girls who Made a Difference:
ISBN 978-1-85792-776-4

Monica of Thagaste, Catherine Luther,
Susanna Wesley, Ann Judson,
Maria Taylor, Susannah Spurgeon,
Bethan Lloyd-Jones,
Edith Schaeffer, Sabina Wurmbrand,
Ruth Bell Graham.

Ten Boys who Made History:
ISBN 978-1-85792-836-5

Charles Spurgeon, Jonathan Edwards,
Samuel Rutherford, D L Moody,
Martin Lloyd-Jones, A W Tozer,
John Owen, Robert Murray McCheyne,
Billy Sunday, George Whitfield.

Ten Girls who Made History:
ISBN 978-1-85792-837-2

Ida Scudder, Betty Green, Jeanette Li,
Mary Jane Kinnaird, Bessie Adams,
Emma Dryer, Lottie Moon,
Florence Nightingale, Henrietta Mears,
Elisabeth Elliot.

LIGHT KEEPERS

Ten Boys who Didn't Give In:
ISBN 978-1-84550-035-1

Polycarp, Alban, Sir John Oldcastle
Thomas Cramer, George Wishart,
James Chalmers, Dietrich Bonhoeffer
Nate Saint, Ivan Moiseyev
Graham Staines.

Ten Girls who Didn't Give In:
ISBN 978-1-84550-036-8

Blandina, Perpetua, Lady Jane Grey,
Anne Askew, Lysken Dirks,
Marion Harvey, Margaret Wilson,
Judith Weinberg, Betty Stam,
Esther John

CHRISTIAN FOCUS PUBLICATIONS

Christian   Christian   CF4K   Mentor
Focus   Heritage

Christian Focus Publications publishes books for adults and children under its four main imprints: Christian Focus, Christian Heritage, CF4K and Mentor. Our books reflect that God's word is reliable and Jesus is the way to know him, and live for ever with him.

Our children's publication list includes a Sunday school curriculum that covers pre-school to early teens; puzzle and activity books. We also publish personal and family devotional titles, biographies and inspirational stories that children will love.

If you are looking for quality Bible teaching for children then we have an excellent range of Bible story and age specific theological books.

From pre-school to teenage fiction, we have it covered!

Find us at our web page:
www.christianfocus.com